WARSAW

BY
LILIANA OLCHOWIK-ADAMOWSKA AND TOMASZ ŁAWECKI

Produced by
Thomas Cook Publishing

Original title: Warszawa
Original text © 2005 Hachette Livre Polska sp. z o.o.
Original maps © 2005 Hachette Livre Polska sp. z o.o.

Written by Liliana Olchowik-Adamowska and Tomasz Ławecki

Original Photography and design by Grzegorz Wilk

Polish-English translation by Blanka Myszkowska and Robert
G. Barker

Page layout by Studio 183, 6 Park Farm, Sandpit Road, Thorney,
Peterborough PE6 OS7.

Published by Thomas Cook Publishing
A division of Thomas Cook Tour Operations Limited
PO Box 227, The Thomas Cook Business Park, Unit 15/16,
Coningsby Road, Peterborough PE3 8SB, United Kingdom

Email: books@thomascook.com
www.thomascookpublishing.com
+44 (0) 1733 416477

ISBN-13: 978-1-84157-492-9
ISBN-10: 1-84157-492-9

Translation © 2006 Thomas Cook Publishing
First edition of the English version © 2006 Thomas Cook Publishing

Printed and bound in Spain by: Grafo Industries Gráficas, Basauri
Front cover credits: left © Alamy; centre © Getty Images; right © Alamy
Back cover credits: © Hachette Livre & Grzegorz Wilk

Contents

KEY TO MAPS

✈   Airport

★   Start of walk

Ⓜ   Metro Station

Introduction

Warsaw spans both banks of the Vistula (Wisła) river and is Poland's main cultural and political centre. The numerous occupations and Second World War destruction have reduced the number of historical sights but the surviving architectural gems and the city's vitality still draw the vistors.

It is often said that East and West meet in Warsaw, and to some extent they do. The two halves of this city, divided by the Vistula River, or *Wisła*, are certainly different. The left bank is dynamic and modern whilst the right remains more traditional; the quarter known as *Praga* has even preserved for itself a little of the notoriety provided by the pre-war underworld.

For many years, Warsaw has pulled in the young and ambitious from all corners of Poland. This is understandable if you consider the vast range of institutions based in the city, while newly founded companies are rapidly expanding, even as the logos of traditional companies reclaim the streets. It may also be said, though not quite in jest, that the prettiest women in Warsaw are those arriving in these migratory waves. This is due to the city's relatively few original families. Many lost all during the 1944 *Warsaw Uprising* (*Powstanie Warszawski; see p14-5*) and had no reason to return to the ruins, while many lived in fear of political repression. For such people it was easier to depart and begin a new life in western Europe, or in the so-called *Recovered Territories*, that is those lands in the western third of the country or north-east that were returned to Poland after the Second World War.

The beauty or otherwise of the Polish capital itself is a controversial issue. Some say that the city's current aspect is indeed a reflection of its great history, despite the near-total wartime destruction and later reconstruction. However, this reflection cannot hope to be a mirror image: the achievement of an identical form being clearly impossible. In fact, post-war architects faced a crippling dilemma: to build an entirely new city from the ground up or reconstruct according to the historical plan. Sadly, no consensus was reached, meaning that both approaches have made their mark on the modern cityscape. Many prominent landmarks were rebuilt early on, for example the Old City (*Starówka*) although its present day form does differ from that of its pre-war days. In enrolling the *Starówka* on UNESCO's World Heritage List, admiration was expressed for both post-war and contemporary construction work. The quarter's architecture harks back to the towns of the first Dukes of Mazovia, as well as to the era of the first Polish kings who made Warsaw their capital.

There are strong arguments for the reconstruction. Warsaw's tempestuous history had made it a symbol, even an icon, of Poland, with successive national uprisings having begun within the city. Sadly, in the immediate aftermath of the war, the Polish capital was a necropolis formed of mountains of debris, yet it could not be abandoned, and the reconstruction of *Warszawa* became a matter of honour and national pride.

Many monuments have been restored or reconstructed in painstaking detail, and these are complemented with new buildings framed by those townhouses which miraculously survived. Dozens of formerly empty squares are fast appearing, with new and handsome skyscrapers sprouting out all over.

Modern architecture suits the new face of Warsaw, which despite its late start and the fact that it accidentally become capital, is proving that the title of first city of Poland is deserved. Warsaw owes this, second rebirth to its incredible vitality. Once a sleepy provincial Russian town, it was transformed into the 'Paris of the North' prior to the outbreak of war in

1939; reborn of ashes it became a grey city hidden behind the Iron Curtain. At present, it is changing again, swiftly evolving into a European centre for politics, commerce and entertainment. Many cultural events, such as the F. Chopin International Piano Contest and the Jazz Jamboree are now coming to the attention of the world. Newer events, such as Summer Jazz Days are becoming fixtures on the international calendar, raising the city's profile further. Behind their success are the receptive and novelty-hungry Varsovians, who neither lose themselves in regret nor look back with anger.

Remember that Warsaw is a city of profound character and a reading of history is worthwhile preparation; in the walls of old buildings bullet craters are still visible, while on many streets grey boards may be seen, each a site of executions. In the hustle and bustle of Warsaw's daily life reflection may seem impossible, yet flowers are placed by those boards and candles are lit.

The City

Genius loci *n. the guardian spirit attributed to a particular place* – which may be felt right here in Warsaw, in the region of Mazovia. The city's peculiar characteristics are founded on the unparalleled energy and imagination which have accompanied its inhabitants through the ages, and which allowed them to live through the periodic crises that have affected the city.

The monument to Prince Józef Poniatowski

Warsaw sprawls over the terraces of the Vistula river, where much geographical charm is provided by the Varsovian Scarp (*Skarpa Warszawska*): the slope of a post-glacial valley, now lined by the Royal Tract (*Trakt Królewski*) and home to the Old Town.

The city's history began in about 1300 when the Duke of Mazovia, Boleslaus II (*Bolesław II*), recognised the defensible nature of the area and moved his court here. This led to the establishment of a town called Warsza. Next, when King Sigismund I 'the Old' (*Zygmunt I Stary*) arrived in Poland in 1526 to assume the rule of Poland, Warsaw was a lesser town within his kingdom, although one enjoying special rights and privileges, powerful defensive walls and a Gothic castle. At that time Krakow was the capital, yet it began to slip in importance after the Polish-Lithuanian Union in 1569, before finally becoming a provincial town. Meanwhile Warsaw, owing to its central location and political importance, grew in stature.

After the childless death of the last king of the Jagiellonian dynasty, Sigismund II Augustus (*Zygmunt II August*) in 1572,

Polish kings began to be elected from amongst European princes on the special 'electoral field' in the village of Wielka Wola, now a quarter of Warsaw. Sigismund III Vasa (*Zygmunt III Waza*), a descendant of both the Polish Jagiellonian and Swedish Vasa dynasties, was elected by this means in 1587, with the ambition of obtaining the crown of Sweden in tandem. Importantly for Warsaw, repairs to Krakow's Wawel castle, Sigismund's usual residence, led him to move temporarily to Warsaw's castle, that of the Dukes of Mazovia. He delayed his return so long that Warsaw was declared the new royal residence.

Those who sought recognition or representation, such as the magnates, church hierarchy, foreign deputies and noblemen, were required to attend the conventions of the Diet (*Sejm*) and the king's court, this in turn leading to the construction of a mass of palaces, manor houses and simpler porch-fronted houses in and around Warsaw. By royal edict, private territories known as *jurydyki* were established, free from both municipal and judicial authority. Warsaw was eventually united as a single homogenous organism

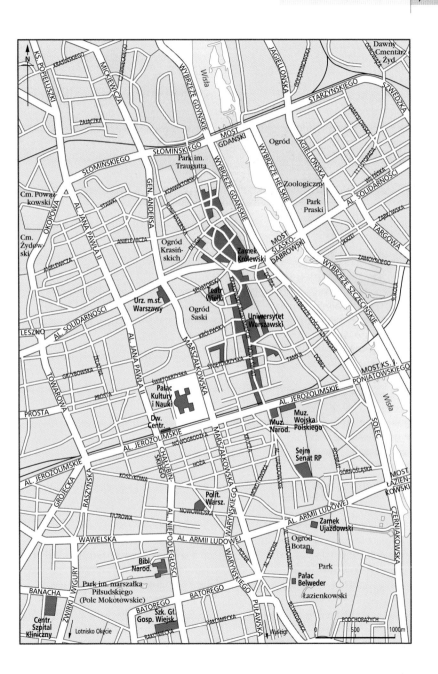

The fountain in the Saski Garden (*Ogród Saski*)

in the 18th century.

On 2nd December 1789, burghers dressed in official black costumes marched from Warsaw's Old Town Market Square (*Rynek Starego Miasta*) to the Royal Castle (*Zamek Królewski*), presenting to the king a memorandum with a claim for reforms. These postulates became part of the Constitution of 3rd May announced at the Royal Castle in 1791, which made all citizens equal and reinforced the role of the state. It was one of the three most progressive constitutions of the time, along with the French Revolutionary constitution (also 1791) and the American constitution (1787).

During this time, in fact from 1772 onwards, a weakened Poland was torn apart by her stronger neighbours, the Russian, Prussian and Austrian empires, in a series of three Partitions that led to the complete disappearance of the country as an independent entity. Hopes of freedom were revived on the Vistula with the arrival of Napoleon Bonaparte in 1807, who established the Duchy of Warsaw. However, after his defeat and the Congress of Vienna in 1815, Warsaw

became the capital city of the puppet Congress Kingdom ruled by the Russian tsars from Moscow. These were hard times of 'russification', when in Warsaw the landscape was altered by the Byzantine copulas of Orthodox churches, the Citadel (*Cytadela*) was built and the city barracks were enlarged.

Poland won its independence in 1918, after the Great War (1914-18), yet in August 1920 the Polish army was again on the defensive, breaking the march of the Soviet Red Army into Europe. The Battle of Warsaw, won by Polish forces on 15th August 1920, is regarded as one of eighteen battles that decided the fate of the world.

The most illustrious Mayor of Warsaw, Stefan Starzyński (in office 1935-39), was a visionary and a perfect manager. He inspired and accomplished the grand plan for Warsaw's 'europeanisation', promoting new investment and activities to improve the city's image. Dozens of parks, squares and avenues were laid out, together with, Starzyński's pride, the broad Independence Avenue, and an underground railway was even designed, although the city would have to wait 60 more years for its construction.

The development of the capital was impressive. The population increased by 70 percent to 1.3 million in 1939. New flats and even new quarters, such as *Żoliborz*, were built, the water supply and transport networks were developed. Streets received asphalt surfaces, a new airport was built and a tunnel for trains was run alongside the city's main artery, Jerozolimskie Avenue.

Just before the Second World War, Warsaw occupied 14,000 hectares, had 1,800 streets and approximately 29,000 buildings, including 900 of historical value. There was also a convenient transportation system, five bridges and several viaducts. Entertainment was provided by bathing areas in the *Praga* quarter, by boat cruises on the Vistula and in roller-skating halls in *Dolinka Szwajcarska*. The cinema was popular, yet theatres, the opera and operettas, dancing, cafés and summer gardens were also a source of delight. Despite the demands of work, play went on into the morning sunshine; the city never slept. This was pre-war Warsaw.

Warsaw was bombed for the first time on 1st September 1939. The German army reached the outskirts on 8th September. The capital was defended by hastily constructed barricades, but after twenty days of one-sided fighting Warsaw surrendered. Mayor Stefan Starzyński had inspired the populace in its defence every day over the radio but was arrested by the Gestapo and died in the potassium mine at Baelberge on 19th March 1944.

The German occupiers were well prepared in their assault on the city and

Warsaw might have always suffered 90 percent destruction; then in 1944, after the failure of the Warsaw Uprising, the order was given to level the city entirely. In the demolition that followed, fortune smiled once; in the heaped ruins, a part of the Saski Palace colonnade survived (*see p55*). This now forms the Tomb of the Unknown Soldier (*Grób Nieznanego Żołnierza*).

On 17th January 1945, the Soviet Army arrived to liberate this most damaged of European cities. As a result of war about 700,000 of Warsaw's inhabitants died, 175,000 were injured or sick, 375,000 were transported to Germany for slave labour and 90,000 transported to concentration camps. The city was 70 percent ruined on the left bank of the Vistula River and about 30 percent on the right. There was no water, no electricity, no transportation, and no telephone communication. From basements buried in rubble, groups of so-called Robinsons emerged; desperados, who refused the order to abandon the city and miraculously survived its destruction.

The Świętokrzyski Bridge (*Most Świętokrzyski*) spans the Vistula River

History

13th-14th century	Post-Lithuanian invasion of Jazdów, the Mazovian capital moves to a safer place on the Varsowian Scarp.
15th century	Suburban development and construction of defensive walls begins. The New Town (*Nowe Miasto*) is founded.
1526	The last Duke of Mazovia dies, the Duchy of Mazovia is incorporated into Poland.
1569	The Polish-Lithuanian Union fuses both countries under one jointly elected king. Warsaw to host convocations of the Polish-Lithuanian Diet.
1573	First permanent bridge over the Vistula is built. Warsaw becomes the site of free royal elections.

The Baroque palace in Wilanów, summer residence of King John III Sobieski

1598–1619	Suburban development continues. The local castle is re-modelled as the royal seat.
1644	First Column of King Sigismund III Vasa (*Kolumna Zygmunta*) built.
17th century	Around Warsaw private territories are established, independent of municipal and judicial authority.
1655–58	The united armies of the Swedish and Hungarian kings, Gustavus X Augustus and György I Rákóczi, ruin Warsaw during the Polish-Swedish war known as the Deluge (*Potop*) and the Rákóczi Invasion.
1677–96	Warsaw develops culturally and economically. The new residence of King John III Sobieski (*Jan III Sobieski*) is built at Wilanów.
1713–30	King August II Wettin (*August II Mocny*), founds the Saxonian Axis which includes the Saski Palace (*Pałac Saski*) and its park.
1764–94	Warsaw is developed in the Classical style and becomes the centre of the Polish Enlightenment.

1770 The Commission of Good Order builds an embankment to demarcate the town limits.

1772 Partition of Poland. Russia, Prussia and Austria take possession of 29 percent of Polish lands and 35 percent of the nation.

1791 The Constitution of 3rd May is passed in Warsaw. The first constitution in Europe and the second in the world, it is the foundation of the modern country's development and a unifying force in terms of administration. It gives new rights of self-governance. Warsaw is divided into six districts.

1793 Second Partition of Poland. Prussia takes about 58,000km² and 1.1m people, Russia 250,000km² and 3m people.

1794 The Kościuszko Uprising begins, aimed at the foreign invaders. Insurgents, led by shoemaker Jan Kiliński and butcher Józef Sierakowski, fight successfully with the Russians in the streets. On 5th November, General A. Suvorov conquers the district and the slaughter the inhabitants of the *Praga* quarter begins.

The Constitution of 3rd May was passed here in the Senator's Hall of the Royal Castle

1795	Third Partition of Poland. Warsaw is divided between Prussia and Russia. Poland disappears from the map until 1918.
1796–1806	Napoleon Bonaparte's army liberates Warsaw.
1807–13	Warsaw made capital of the Duchy of Warsaw, founded by Napoleon.
1815–30	After the Congress of Vienna, Warsaw becomes capital of the Kingdom of Poland, a Russian dependency with limited autonomy.
1830–31	The November Uprising against Russia begins. Warsaw witnesses an attack on the Belvedere and battles in neighbouring *Olszynka Grochowska* and *Wawer*, now districts of the city.
1845	First length of the Warsaw-Vienna railroad line is opened.
1853–56	The re-building of the streets continues, while the first water supply system is laid out and gas lanterns illuminate the city.
1859–64	Kierbedź's Bridge is constructed, the city's first of steel.

1863–64	The January Uprising
1901	The National Philharmonic (*Filharmonia Narodowa*) is opened.
1907	The first electric trams appear in the streets.
1915–18	During the Great War, the city falls under German occupation. War pushes the economy into crisis.
1920	A battle, the Miracle of the Vistula, is fought on 15th August on fields near Warsaw, the Polish army defeats the Bolsheviks.
1935–39	Warsaw grows rapidly under Mayor Stefan Starzyński.
1939	The German invasion of Poland begins the Second World War. Warsaw is bombed from 1st September to 28th October. The Germans proclaim the *General Gubernia*, the unit for administrating part of the Polish territory.
1940–42	Germans organise deportations from Warsaw to the concentration camps. The Jewish ghetto is established and Jews are deported to the gas chambers of Treblinka.

Polish Underground State organises various attacks and acts of sabotage.

1943 Jewish Ghetto Uprising begin on 19th April. 60,000 Jews killed.

1944 The Warsaw Uprising begins on 1st August, planned by the Polish Home Army. After 63 days of fighting, leaders sign an honourable capitulation. An estimated 650,000 inhabitants are killed, with the remainder exiled from the city. Nazis demolish the city house by house, even burning libraries and valuable collections. About 84 percent of the city centre lies in ruins.

1945 The Soviet Red Army liberates Warsaw.

1955 Eastern Bloc countries sign the Warsaw Pact. Warsaw receives the Palace of Science and Culture as a gift from the Soviet Union.

1956 After the death of Stalin the 'Thaw' begins in Poland. Władysław Gomułka becomes First Secretary of the Polish United Workers' Party (PZPR).

1979 Polish Pope, John Paul II, makes first pilgrimage to

his homeland.

1980 The Independent Self-governing Trade Union known as Solidarity (*NSZZ 'Solidarnoœæ'*) is founded in Gdańsk, the new movement spreading quickly across Poland.

1981 General W. Jaruzelski proclaims Martial Law. Solidarity activists are arrested.

1984 Hundreds of Varsovians gather at the funeral of Warsaw metallurgists' chaplain, Jerzy Popiełuszko, killed by the Security Service on 13th October.

1989 The Round Table Debates commence. Tadeusz Mazowiecki becomes the first Prime Minister following free elections.

1999 Poland joins NATO.

2004 Poland becomes a member of the EU.

The uprising broke out on 1st August 1944 at 5pm. It might have lasted for only forty eight hours, perhaps even for a few weeks, but in fact it continued for two whole months. The German occupiers gathered special forces, obliterated point after point of resistance, demolished the city quarter-by-quarter and murdered civilians. Warsaw suffered a shortage of medicines as well as a lack of food for civilians and ammunition for the rebels.

The uprising ended with capitulation in Ożarów on 2nd October 1944. The Nazis deported rebels to camps, while surviving inhabitants were exiled and the ruins razed to the ground.

It is only in the last few years that

this 'forgotten uprising' has been set in its rightful place within the popular mind. The uprising's 60th anniversary was attended by a great number of dignitaries from those countries allied with Poland during the war, and also among them, the German Chancellor.

In the former tram depot on Przyokopowa Street in the *Wola* quarter, the Museum of the Warsaw Uprising (*Muzeum Powstania Warszawskiego*) has been founded. Audio-visual media recalls the atmosphere of insurrectionary Warsaw and there are relics of the days of the rebellion. Particularly telling is a wall, listing the names of those insurgents killed in the fighting.

As you walk though the modern city, the landscape of those dark days may still be conjured up. A barricade of trams stood on Wolska Street, not far from the Museum, its fall heralding the bloody pacification of the Wola quarter. The landmark Waszawa Hotel, on the corner of Świętokrzyska and Powstańców Warszawy Square (*Plac Powstańców Warszawy*), was famous for being the highest skyscraper of the pre-war capital and was conquered by the rebels as early as 2nd August - the Polish flag was raised there. The PAST building on Zielna Street was a well-armed nest of Nazi resistance and came under sustained attack before finally being conquered a few days later.

The pavements of the Old Town also saw much and can speak volumes. The rebels controlled the area from the Old Town to Bielańska Street, where the head office of the Polish Bank once stood, yet today is in ruins. It was here that their unsuccessful push towards the city centre began. The Old Town was isolated. Earlier, a stiff struggle took place at St John the Baptists Cathedral (*Katedra św. Jana*), where German soldiers gained entry by detonating the tank-mine known as 'Goliath' inside; the caterpillar tracks of the Goliath have been affixed to the south wall of the re-built cathedral. A plaque on Kilińskiego Street remembers victims of a trap involving a mechanized combat vehicle, inside which a bomb was planted, left on the street by the Germans. The ruse worked well, the vehicle killing the many bystanders who gathered to see what they believed to be a harmless trophy. A monument to the Warsaw Uprising stands on Krasińskis Square (*see Monuments p106-7*), an original manhole cover placed on the lawn beside it in memory of rebels evacuated from the Old Town through the sewer system.

The uprising enjoyed glorious days, when entire streets were liberated from the occupiers. But bitter days of defeat would follow as houses were left by night in impossible conditions, their residents escaping underground from the lost districts.

It was a time of heroism, of small pleasures, youthful friendship and even love; the rebels were predominantly young, many very young. Those child-rebels are commemorated today in a monument to the 'Little Insurgent' (below).

Left: the PAST building; Top: *Kubuś*, the vehicle used by the rebels

Governance

The first capital of Poland was Gniezno, the second Krakow and the third Warsaw. Key to the latter's ascendancy was its central location and the foreign policies of kings elected in free elections. Despite damage and its reduction to a provincial town, Warsaw preserved its regal character and its status as the greatest political centre of Poland.

Convention of the Citizens' platform (PO)

Warsaw, a lesser settlement of Mazovia, came by its modern significance in the mid-16th century. In 1569 the Polish Diet (*Sejm*) took the decision to hold Polish-Lithuanian conventions in Warsaw following validation of the Polish-Lithuanian Union, which bound both countries together as one entity. It was also decided that convocations of the Diet and free royal elections would take place in Warsaw. The foreign policy of elected kings, Stefan Bathory (*Stefan Batory*) and Sigismund III Vasa (*Zygmunt III Waza*), determined that Warsaw was to be a residential town. Ruling from Warsaw rather than more southerly Krakow was easier for wars fought in the northern and eastern territories. Sigismund III Vasa, whose lineage lay with the Swedish royal family, transferred his court to Warsaw from Krakow in 1611, not only owing to political circumstances, but also due to a fire at Krakow's Wawel castle in 1596. However, it took until 1795 for the new status of Warsaw as His Majesty's residence to be acknowledged.

As the capital, Warsaw was to witness a number of fierce military confrontations. The city was completely destroyed in the period of the Swedish Deluge, that is the Polish-Swedish war in the mid-17th century, and again during the 19th-century uprisings, when bloody struggles were fought. Over the one hundred years of Partition, Warsaw developed economically yet remained politically dependent. Only in 1918, when Poland had regained independence and the need for a capital returned, did Warsaw again become the centre of national politics.

The Second World War brought 80 percent destruction but despite this, the municipal authority opted not to move the functions of the capital elsewhere; clearance of the piles of rubble was undertaken immediately after the war, by Varsovians in their thousands.

Today, Warsaw is the main political centre of Poland. The Presidential Palace (*Pałac Prezydencki*) is the seat of the President of Poland, who is elected every five years in a free election. The President may veto legislation and is also responsible for the appointment of the Prime Minister, whose seat is on Ujazdowskie Avenues (*Aleje Ujazdowskie*). Wiejska Street hosts the legislative, two-chamber Diet (*Sejm*) which is chosen every four years in a general election.

Warsaw is a meeting place for politicians from all corners of the world and the place where national holidays, festivities and commemorations are celebrated with foreign delegates. Special security measures are put in place for international meetings of high ranking participants, which can cause difficulties and even prevent the flow of traffic along the Royal Tract (*Trakt Królewski*) or Żwirki i Wigury Avenue (*Aleja Żwirki i Wigury*), leading to Okęcie Airport (*Lotnisko Okęcie*). Residents do not hide their dissatisfaction at this, but they are certainly proud when Warsaw makes the front pages.

Warsaw is also home to local authorities. The municipal legislative body is the sixty-member Council of the Capital City of Warsaw. The Mayor of Warsaw is elected in direct elections, has administrative power and is responsible for the realisation of all activities. The mayoral seat is on Bankowy Square (*Plac Bankowy*) in the building that flies a yellow and red flag, although some departments of the Municipal Office are unfortunately spread over a number of locations. Some are to be found in the Palace of Science and Culture (*Pałac Kultury i Nauki*), some in the Azure Skyscraper (*Błękitny Wieżowiec*) and others the Branickis palace (*Pałac Branickich*) on Miodowa Street. However, the authorities do plan to build a new City Hall capable of hosting all of these departments under one roof.

Warsaw is divided into eighteen boroughs; *Bemowo, Białołęka, Bielany, Mokotów, Ochota, South Praga, North Praga, Rembertów, Śródmieście* (City Centre), *Targówek, Ursus, Ursynów, Wawer, Wesoła, Wilanów, Włochy, Wola* and *Żoliborz*. Although administration is centralised, each borough has its own mayor chosen by a borough council. For more information on Warsaw's organisational structure and management take a look at www.e-warsaw.pl.

This building on Krasińskich Square hosts the courts

Geography

Warsaw lies in the Varsovian Valley on the banks of the longest Polish river, the Vistula. The Varsovian Valley is part of the Mazovia-Podlasie Lowland, which is in turn part of the Land of Great Valleys (*Kraina Wielkich Dolin*). The Land of Great Valleys is itself one vast expanse in the vaster Great European Plain stretching from the Atlantic Ocean to the Ural Mountains deep within Russia. Warsaw's is a mild climate: the average annual temperature does not exceed 8°C, the average temperature for July is over 18°C.

The French garden, the palace in Wilanów

Warsaw's geographic location is a rather unfavourable one in the sense that there are no natural defensive barriers. Along the north-south axis, between the Kampinoska Woodland (*Puszcza Kampinoska*) and Chojnowskie Forest (*Lasy Chojnowskie*), there are no natural obstructions to airflow and so the city is wonderfully oxygenated and does not experience smog. It is also worthy of note that Warsaw is the only European capital to have a national park for a neighbour. The Kampinoski National Park lies adjacent to the northern limits of the Bielany district. The southern part butts up against the town of Konstancin-Jeziorna, a fashionable health resort since the 1920s and 30s with a scenic Spa Park (*Park Zdrojowy*) and 'graduation towers' invented to harness the therapeutic powers of evaporating brine waters.

The largest body of water in the Warsaw area is the Zegrzyński Impoundment Lake (*Zalew Zegrzyński*; 30km northeast of the city centre), formed when the Narew River was dammed in 1963 near Dębe. With an area of 33km², the lake is now a popular watersports centre and place of recreation.

The Kurpiowska Woodland (*Puszcza Kurpiowska*; about 100km from Warsaw) is located in the northeastern part of the Mazovia region and is famous for traditional religious customs and an unusually rich folklore. In the more immediate surroundings of Warsaw, dozens of palaces formerly belonging to magnates, and porch-fronted manors owned by the nobility, have survived.

The attractive landscapes of the Varsovian Valley are the creation of the last unregulated European river, the Vistula. Warsaw is located on the terraces of the Vistula's banks, at the point where they form the so-called Varsovian Scarp. The height of the Scarp in the Old Town area is 114m, while the width of the Vistula varies from place to place.

Economy

The population of Warsaw is about 1,690,000, spread over an area of 516.9km². After the Upper Silesian conurbation formed around Katowice, this is the second largest agglomeration of people in Poland and the nation's largest city-based industrial centre.

Recently established industrial blocs have undergone huge transformations in ownership. For instance, the Warsaw Ironworks was bought by Italian concerns, the car factory in the Żerań quarter is awaiting a new investor after the bankruptcy of Daewoo, the chocolate-maker E. Wedel was first bought by Pepsi-Co and later acquired by the British company Cadbury, while Pollena Cosmetics was bought by Cussons Group Ltd.

Warsaw is still the centre of the electronics, electrical and publishing industries, along with electricity generation and well-developed centres of the chemical, mechanical, food, metal, fuel, clothing and iron industries. All of the city's factories have been modernised and are located in the peripheral districts so as not to endanger the Warsaw's ecology. In addition, they are surrounded by extensive forests and located on an open plain, helping to make Warsaw as well oxygenated as possible.

Service industries such as trading and repairs are the most common branch of small business activity, equalling 30.9 percent of the total. Second place, totalling 26 percent, is real estate management and the financial services. Warsaw offers 219 banks and a huge number of modern office complexes in a selection of newly built skyscrapers.

Quarters

The most interesting quarter for the visitor is *Śródmieście*, or city centre, whose central point is located at the junction of Marszałkowska Street and Jerozolimskie Avenue. This busy communications hub has the Palace of Culture and Science, huge shopping centres and the *Centrum* underground station. The *Śródmieście* also covers the length of Jerozolimskie Avenue with its two railway stations; *Śródmieście* and *Centralny*, and with the Polish Airways (LOT) terminal and a range of renowned hotels. Chałubińskiego Street and Jana Pawła II Avenue have become a new business centre, built up with modern office complexes.

The Old Town, Krakowskie Przedmieście Street and Nowy Świat Street, together with two squares, Teatralny and Piłsudskiego, form the city's cultural centre. The southern part of the Royal Tract (*Trakt Królewski*) is an area of embassies and parks, the Tract reaching as far as the Palace and Park of *Wilanów* and the recreational areas in *Powsin*.

Other quarters worth mentioning are the southern *Mokotów*, western *Wola*, peaceful *Żoliborz*, green *Bielany*, commercial *Ochota*, and *Praga*, the heart of local folklore.

A traffic jam on Bankowy Square

People and Culture

When Sigismund III Vasa moved the capital from Krakow to Warsaw the town grew in importance, with the political and cultural life of the country concentrating here right up to the present day. Warsaw is home to a number of theatres, cinemas and museums, while international exhibitions are organised and a range of festivals attract world-famous artists. The diverse schedule of events held in the city are aimed at both Polish and foreign guests.

A bookstore

Once Warsaw became home to the royal court in the late 16th century, it developed into the main centre of Polish cultural life. At the turn of the 16th and 17th centuries, plenty of new buildings sprang up in Warsaw, among them the Royal Castle (*Zamek Królewski*), constructed and decorated with the assistance of Italian artists Giovani Trevano, Matteo Castelli, Constantino Tencalla and Matteo Trapola. Also working in Poland was the illustrious Dutch architect Tylman van Gameren, who designed the magnificent Krasińskis Palace (*Pałac Krasińskich*) and the Benedictine

The play *Served the King of England* by B Hrabal at the Dramatyczny Theatre

Church of Perpetual Adoration of the Blessed Sacrament (*Kościół Sakramentek*).

In the 18th century, artists both Polish and from abroad, such as the Italians Pompeo Ferrari and Francesco Placidi found rich patrons in Warsaw. When the court of King August II Wettin (*August II Mocny*) was welcomed from Saxony in Germany, Warsaw also took in the Saxon artists Johann Friedrich Knöbel and Matthäus Daniel Pöppelman. The loss of independence and the dark period after the November Uprising (*Powstanie Listopadowe*, 1830-31) brought about a wave of emigration to France, such remarkable artists as the composer Fryderyk Chopin and the romantic poets Kamil Norwid and Zygmunt Krasiński being forced to leave their homeland.

The late 19th century and the early 20th century was the period of great Varsovian writers. These included the Nobel Prize winners Henryk Sienkiwicz and Władysław Reymont and the novelist and feuilletonist Bolesław Prus. Władysław Reymont, who received his award for the novel *The Pheasants* (*Chłopi*), spent almost his whole life in Warsaw. The young Reymont attended tailoring courses at the House of Handicraft (*Dom Rzemiosła*), No. 14 Miodowa Street, and the inscription on the commemorative plaque at No. 41 Krakowskie Przedmieście Street reads: 'Władysław Stanisław Reymont, master tailor, Noble Prize laureate.'

The 'Paris of the North', as Warsaw was known between the wars (1918-1939), was the home of one of the best European cabarets, *Qui pro Quo*, the scripts for which were written by one of the greatest Polish poets, Julian Tuwim, while Hungarian Fryderyk Járosy was the director and compère. The onset of the Second

The monument to Marshal Józef Piłsudski

World War, however, would end the show. Symptomatically, just before the outbreak of war Witold Gombrowicz, the author of the drama *Ferdydurke*, departed Warsaw where he was working, for Argentina. Today, however, the cultural traditions of pre-war Warsaw are being built upon in opera, theatre and cabaret, and the atmosphere of the pre-war city has returned in literature and film.

Pre-war Warsaw is described in the masterpieces of prose written in the Yiddish language by Issac Bashevis Singer, who lived in Krochmalna Street for many years before emmigrating to the USA in 1935. Shortly after he began writing in America he received the Nobel Prize. In his novels and stories, the author of *The Magician of Lublin* portrayed the life of the Jewish community and drew the cultural plan of the pre-war capital. Singer's books would have served as superb guidebooks to Warsaw had the city not been so damaged in the Warsaw Uprising of 1944.

Film director Roman Polański, currently living in Paris, recalls the tragic period of Warsaw's German occupation in the film *The Pianist* (*Pianista*). His first films were produced in Poland and he also staged Peter Shaffer's *Amadeus* at the *Teatr na Woli*. *The Pianist* is the true story of a Polish musician of Jewish origin, Władysław Szpilman, and was shot in surviving tenement buildings as well as at reconstructed locations. In 2003, the film was awarded several Oscar statuettes, with Polański himself receiving the most precious for direction.

Contemporary Warsaw hosts numerous cultural events throughout the year, hits including the annual *A Mozart Festival* (*Festiwal Mozartowski*) and the *Old Music*

Cartouche at the entrance of an Old Town house

Festival (*Festiwal Muzyki Dawnej*). Musicians and audience alike experience a particularly charged atmosphere during the F Chopin International Piano Contest (*Międzynarodowy Konkurs Pianistyczny im. F.Chopina*), which is organised only once every five years.

The National Philharmonic (*Filharmonia Narodowa*) has played host to the F Chopin International Piano Contest since 1927. Every five years, young pianists from around the world arrive in the city of Chopin's youth, and indeed half of his life. The jury consists of famous virtuosos and the performers play only Chopin's compositions. Victory opens the door to world-renowned philharmonics, and often international, career. Future contests will be held in 2005, 2010 and 2015.

Concerts of Chopin's music, held in the most beautiful gardens of *Łazienki*, have become a popular post-war tradition in Warsaw. They are organised from spring to autumn, always on a Sunday at noon, and take place at the bandstand by the Secession (Art Nouveau) monument, which was chiselled for the composer by Wacław Szymanowski. For fans of more modern forms of music, the most important event is perhaps the Warsaw Autumn International Festival of Contemporary Music (*Międzynarodowy Festiwal Muzyki Współczesnej Warszawska Jesień*). Jazz lovers have their Jazz Jamboree, also in autumn, which has taken place in Warsaw since 1958 and is one of the most important jazz festivals in Europe. It is held at the Congress Hall of the Palace of Culture and Science (*Sala Kongresowa Pałacu Kultury i Nauki*) and has hosted all these jazz greats: Ray Charles, Ella Fitzgerald, Miles Davis and Stan Getz.

Polish musicians also play at the Jazz Jamboree. Past concerts have been given by Krzysztof Komeda-Trzciński, the creator of the music for the Roman Polański film *Rosemary's Baby*, by the saxophonist Włodzimierz Nahorny, also by America's top-ranking virtuoso violinist Michał Urbaniak, and by the successful singer Urszula Dudziak, who lives in New York.

In the largest concert hall in the city, the Congress Hall of the Palace of Culture and Science (*Sala Kongresowa Pałacu Kultury i Nauki*), jazz, blues, pop or rock can be heard daily. As well as playing host to concerts featuring international stars, the Congress Hall welcomes concerts through the *Summer Jazz Days* festival. For 50 years it has been the site of all manner of events, conferences, jubilee celebrations and international trade fairs.

An essential element of the Warsaw skyline is the monumental building of the Great Theatre (*Teatr Wielki*), which also embraces the Polish National Opera (*Opera Narodowa*) with its huge performances of the world's finest operas. The Great Theatre is also forever etched into the history of Poland ever since, in March

1968, the authorities of the communist regime ordered the removal of the posters for *Forefathers' Eve* (*Dziady*) directed by Kazimierz Dejmek, an action that led to students taking to the streets. (*see p53*)

Smaller and no less attractive among the capital's stages are the Warsaw Chamber Opera (*Warszawska Opera Kameralna*) and the *Współczesny, Powszechny* and *Dramatyczny* theatres, the latter home to the annual *Meetings* theatre festival. The city's other theatres are the *Rozmaitości, Syrena* and *Studio Buffo*, not to mention the original *Scena Prezentacje* located in an old factory.

Film fans have both huge multiplex and underground cinemas to choose from, while the most significant cinematic event is the Warsaw International Film Festival, which showcases dozens of films from all corners of the world.

Warsaw's cultural character can only be truly appreciated when the collections of the city's museums are also taken into consideration. The National Museum

The interior of the popular *Tygmont* jazz club

(*Muzeum Narodowe*) possesses Christian frescoes from the Cathedral in Faras, Sudan, while the Museum of the Polish Army (*Muzeum Wojska Polskiego*) and Museum of Technology (*Muzeum Techniki*) offer their own historic wonders. Interesting art exhibitions may be seen at the *Zachęta* National Gallery of Art, and Ujazdowski Castle hosts the trendy Centre for Contemporary Art (*Centrum Sztuki Współczesnej*).

A concert at the National Philharmonic

Warsaw is rich in both historical anecdotes and in legends concerning its beginnings, landmarks and key events.

The City's Foundation

The foundation of Warsaw is enveloped in legend. One such legend involves the townhouse at No. 31 on the Old Market Square (*Rynek Starego Miasta*), known as the Townhouse under the Twins (*Kamienica pod Bliźniętami*) due to its statue of a mother with two babies. In fact, the statue has a typically religious character and portrays St Anna with Mary and the baby Jesus. It is said that one day a prince became lost while out hunting in the forest and that he came across the cottage of a poor but happy family, home to a woodsman who had just become a father of twins. The prince called them *Wars* and *Sawa* and, grateful for the hospitality he was shown, built a manor for the children, thus initiating the construction of *Warszawa*.

Nobody knows the truth of course, but nevertheless *Wars* and *Sawa* are regarded as the mythical founders of Warsaw. A variant on the story tells of two lovers, *Wars* the young fisherman who captures the beautiful mermaid *Sawa* in the waters of Vistula.

Old Town Legends

Many townhouses on the Old Market Square have their own legends. The 16th-century townhouse at No. 27, called the Fukiers' Townhouse (*Kamienica Fukierowska*) or the Townhouse under the Little Roof (*Kamienica pod Daszkiem*), was once in the possession of the wine-trading Fukiers family. At this time, there were complaints of terrible groans coming from the cellars. However, these subsided when the cellars were sealed with a stone. The 19th-century owner, Teofil Florian Fukier was a man with a heart of gold. He played host to writers, painters, actors and actresses in his winery, and his clients included the actress Helena Modrzejwska, the writer Bolesław Prus, the poet Adam Asnyk and the painter Jan Matejko. Jan Matejko was even served by Fukier with wine from the 16th-century barrel, a great honour. Today the cellars have been replaced by the elegant Fukiers' Restaurant where

legend has it those terrible groans can again be heard.

Royal Square Legends

The Column of King Sigismund III Vasa (**Kolumna Zygmunta**) standing near the Royal Castle (**Zamek Królewski**) also has its own legend. It has been observed that whenever Warsaw is endangered, the king raises his hand, the one clasping a sabre. This phenomenon was reportedly witnessed for the first time, during the Kościuszko Uprising in 1794, by rebels from the Old Town led by the shoemaker Jan Kiliński as they advanced on the Russian Army. The combat was overseen from on high by the king. In 1944, when the rebels of the Warsaw Uprising were leaving the Old Town through the sewer system the bronze statue toppled into the ruins of his town. Today the king stands, once more, at peace.

Legends of the Palaces

Warsaw has dozens of palaces previously owned by quite fearsome individuals. One of the first palaces to have a roof of metal plates, the so-called Palace under Metal Plate (**Pałac pod Blachą**), was owned by Prince Józef Poniatowski, a commander in Napoleon Bonaparte's Army and French Marshal. According to legend, in 1784 Prince Poniatowski successfully swam the River Elbe wearing full armour, only to be given the portent, 'You have beaten the Elbe yet will die by the magpie.' In 1813 the Prince drowned in the Elster river during the Battle of Leipzig. Elster in German means magpie...

Another story concerns the Baroque Ostrogskis Palace (**Pałac Ostrogskich**), built by Tylman van Gameren. In the subterranean passages of the palace the Gold Duck is rumoured to live: a gold duck who was in fact a princess, under enchantment, who may only be saved by a young shoemaker. One day a shoemaker did set out in search of the duck. He found the duck and was told that to both help her and win great treasure he must fulfil one task. He was given a hundred ducats with the command that he must spend them all in a single night, though only for his pleasure. They were not to be shared with anybody else. The shoemaker had spent all but the last few coins at the bottom of his pockets when, on his way to free the princess from enchantment, he met a begger. Digging deep, he found the last few coins and foolishly handed them over. He had broken the rules, and the Gold Duck still awaits the breaking of the spell. A Gold Duck decorates the fountain by the palace.

Left centre: A mermaid or *Syrenka* – symbol of Warsaw
Bottom left: Mythical basilisk as a signboard of the restaurant *Bazyliszek*
Middle: Gold Duck by the Ostrogskis Palace

First Steps

One of the most frequently visited cities in Poland, Warsaw has recently been improving its image. New hotels and restaurants are being built and tourist organisations offering city tours are in great demand. Beyond this, all of the sights and attractions promoted in tourist information centres or described in information booklets are now easily accessible thanks to better signposting.

A wheeled train tours the Old Town

When to go?

Winter in Warsaw, November to March, is not much fun and is probably not the best time of year to visit. Snow quickly turns into a dirty slush and cleaning crews are not always able to keep the pavements and streets dry and ice-free.

On the other hand, spring in Warsaw is an exceedingly pleasant time when temperatures are almost summery yet not reaching boiling heat, intolerable in a city heavy with traffic. July and August are rarely so scorching as to make sightseeing difficult and you'll find the capital even a little deserted, the native Varsovians having left for their holidays. In addition, there are few traffic jams and dozens of outdoor events taking place at this time.

September and the beginning of October in Poland are advertised as the 'Golden Autumn'; a time when all of the autumnal hues are present in the landscape. This is a rich cultural season too.

Getting Around

As the capital of Poland, Warsaw is the main focus of the national road and rail networks and is therefore easily accessible from every border crossing. Warsaw has three main railway stations, the Western (*Zachodni*) on the border of the *Wola* and *Ochota* quarters, the Eastern (*Wschodni*) in the Praga quarter and the Central (*Centralny*) in the city centre on Jerozolimskie Avenues (*Al. Jerozolimskie*). Central Station (*Dworzec Centralny*) is the largest and is serviced

Interior of *Wierzbno* underground station

by all long-distance trains. Suburban routes, to locations around 100km out, are provided for by a fourth hub, City Centre Station (*Dworzec Śródmieście*). The international airport at Okęcie (*Lotnisko Okęcie*) is compact, but has the advantage of being located within the borders of the city and is connected with the centre by means of the wide, lime tree-lined Żwirki i Wigury Avenue (*al. Żwirki i Wigury*). Local or hotel shuttle buses, which run every half an hour, mean that transport back and forth is no problem.

Warsaw is a sprawling city and certainly not homogeneous, even in the centre, the sole exception to this rule being the Old Town. As such, the city is too large to be traversed on foot in its entirety, although individual districts do suit exploration in this way. At present, the Warsaw underground only has a single line running south to north, but even this makes travel easier. In addition, the city's bus routes form a star-shaped network with good coverage in the city centre; many daytime routes and all night buses intersect at Central Station (*Dworzec Centralny*).

Navigation

Warsaw is quite well signposted, particularly nearer the centre. On the plates bearing street names (street is *ulica* in Polish), the name of the quarter (*dzielnica*) also appears, while the frequent signs marked with blue waves indicate the direction of the Vistula along with its course. This last piece of information is more important than it

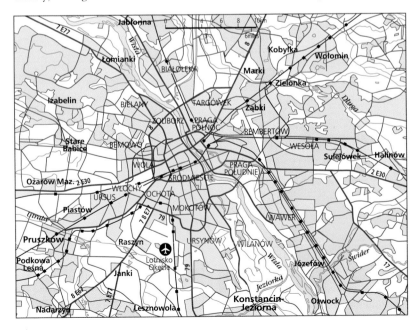

might seem: house numbers rise as they move away from the river on streets that are perpendicular to it, while on streets parallel to the Vistula house numbers rise along its course.

Going by car

Driving a car in the rush hour is a difficult task; visitors travelling in private cars should be aware that drivers in Warsaw do not allow last minute changes of line or stopping to turn. In fact, driving in Warsaw may well be the greatest of challenges for someone accustomed to good road manners. Also, some parts of Warsaw, such as the Old Town, are inaccessible to motorised tourists. The next issue to consider is the prevalence of car thieves. Order is kept by the Police (*Policja*) and the City Guard (*Straż Miejska*); the latter being particularly diligent in issuing tickets for illegal parking and for exceeding the duration of a stay, once it's paid for. Tickets are obtained from parkomats (*parkomat*) and displayed in windscreens.

Busy passage near *Centrum* underground station

Taxis

Taxis in Warsaw are inexpensive. But only use ones topped with a roof lamp marked 'TAXI' and that bear the phone number of a taxi firm. Warsaw suffers from the existence of a 'taxi mafia', so it is best to call for a taxi or to take one that you have seen vacated in front of the Departure Hall. Never take a taxi or accept the invitations of taxi drivers waiting near the airport or railway station. Taxi firms guarantee the quality of their service and offer reasonable prices, and in the event of any problems a complaint can be made.

Sightseeing

The best way to see Warsaw's sights is via the city's public transport network. The perfect choice is the No 180 bus, which begins its route in Wilanów, runs along the whole of the Royal Tract (*Trakt Królewski*) and finishes in the area of the monumental Powązki cemetery (*Cmentarz Powązki*). A journey to the attractions of the Old Town or to the most beautiful of the city's squares will usually be pleasantly short. Buses also run through the ex-Jewish Ghetto and to Okopowa Street (*ul. Okopowa*) home to the Jewish Cemetery (*Cmentarz Żydowski*). Checking the bus timetable in advance is recommended in order to avoid lengthy waits. Tired explorers may rest their legs in the omnipresent pubs and cafés, many of which offer outdoor seating in summer.

Customs

Varsovians are relatively easy-going and pay little attention to fickle fashion. The majority of young people do speak a

Shopping options near the Old town walls

foreign language, most often English, while at the other extreme the elderly may well speak German or Russian. The times when every educated and high-born Pole spoke French now belongs to the realms of history. Despite their fast living, Varsovians can be counted on to treat a visitor with kindness and provide assistance with any problems.

Safety

Warsaw is no less safe than any other European city, yet situations in which problems might arise should of course be avoided insofar as possible. Do not make any accidental friendships or venture out late at night to the lesser-visited parts of the city far from tourist centres and keep your wallet out of sight when not needed.

The cost of living

Warsaw is one of the most expensive cities in Poland. However, in comparison to almost any other European metropolis it is moderately cheap. It is well known that in a hotel restaurant a guest can expect to pay a little more, but prices in the bars, beer gardens and chain restaurants are quite good. Shopping should be done in the malls outside the city, the prices being lower than in the stores on the main streets; the cheapest option of all is the bazaar (*bazar*). The cost of accommodation can seem rather high, yet visitors may occasionally be surprised by weekend discounts or promotions. Warsaw offers a wide variety of standards and prices, and the city has grown richer particularly in terms of two- and three-star hotels.

The Old Town

The Old Town (*Stare Miasto*) was founded at the turn of the 13th and 14th centuries not far away from the old burgh of the Dukes of Mazovia. It is the oldest quarter of Warsaw and has a preserved medieval street plan, its most important building now being the Royal Castle (*Zamek Królewski*), built at the turn of the 16th and 17th centuries on the site of the former wooden burgh.

The clock on the Simonettich House

For almost 400 years the Old Town, which gained its name following post-war restoration, played a vital role in the political and cultural life of the whole country. In the 14th century, the Dukes of Mazovia moved their capital from the *Jazdów* burgh, which had been damaged by Lithuanian invaders, to the current location of the Royal Castle, the old wooden houses being replaced by new brick ones. In 1569, when it became home to the convocations of the common Polish-Lithuanian Diet (see History 1569; p10), Warsaw also became the capital of Poland. The Old Town developed rapidly, with the Varsovian patricians wanting the imposing townhouses on the Market Square (*Rynek*). Later, these patricians would be ousted by rich artists, writers and high-profile politicians.

Nowadays the *Starówka* is a relatively small complex of buildings surrounding the Market Square, the previous complex having been razed during the Second World War. Beginning on the 1st August 1944, the Warsaw Uprising (*Powstanie Warszawskie*) raged for 63 days; during this time the townhouses and churches of the Old Town were the scene of ceaseless combat. The occupying German army reduced the area to ruins; tanks even drove into the St John the Baptist Cathedral (*Katedra św. Jana*) and the churches where the rebels organised makeshift hospitals were bombed. When the uprising had finally been put down the Nazis razed all the buildings still standing.

Between 1948 and 1953 the Old Town was restored to its 18th-century form, with the majority of the unsuitable and disfiguring outbuildings remodelled. Cellars survived the war along with, although rarely, the ground floors of buildings along with their decorative portals. The modern late-Gothic, Renaissance or baroque facades with stucco and sgraffito decoration, as well as the characteristic lanterns, are all the work of the post-war Polish monument preservers. The medieval defensive walls were partially reconstructed and put on display, while St John the Baptist Cathedral (Katedra św. Jana) and Royal Castle (Zamek Królewski) were also restored.

The whole Old Town complex is enrolled on the UNESCO World Heritage List.

Plac Zamkowy (Castle Square)

Castle Square was completed in 1818 and replaced both the courtyard of the previous castle and the old Przedzamkowa Street. The first part of the square was already in existence as early as 1644, the year when construction of the Column of King Sigismund III Vasa (*Kolumna Zygmunta*) was being prepared.

The complex of burger's townhouses was restored after the Second World War. Townhouse No. 19, on the corner, was known as *Pigułczyńska* and was owned by the court musician, architect and poet Adam Jarzębski, who authored the first versed guidebook to Warsaw, published in 1643.

Castle Square is also a window onto a pretty section of Krakowskie Przedmieście Street, where you'll find the attractive Prażmowski Townhouse (No. 87 Krakowskie Przedmieście Street;

Kamienica Prażmowskich). This was built back in the second half of the 17th century by a royal physician named Pastorius but its modern appearance is a result of its remodelling in 1754 by the Leszczyński family, who bought it for the king of Poland and queen of France. The building now belongs to the Polish Writers' Association, and visitors admiring the area of Castle Square and Krakowskie Przedmieście Street are welcomed to the popular café *Literacka*, located on the ground floor.

Kolumna Zygmunta (The Column of King Sigismund III Vasa)

The column standing in the centre of Castle Square is the oldest secular monument in Warsaw and the second oldest in Poland (the first being the statue of Neptune in Gdańsk). The 22m-high monument was built in 1644 by King Ladislas IV Vasa (*Władysław IV*,

Colourful townhouses by the Royal Square

Sigismund's son) and it glorifies Sigismund III Vasa in a way previously reserved only for saints. The structure consists of a granite Corinthian column supported by a plinth and topped with the figure of the king cast in bronze. The king holds the cross in his left hand and a sabre in his right. He is crowned and a richly decorated mantle hangs from his shoulders.

The column evokes to the legend of the king, raising his sabre before battle to inspire bravery. Italians, Augustus Locci and Constantino Tencalla, who served at the court of Ladislas IV Vasa, designed the column and Clemente Molli was sculptor. Enrico Marconi designed the base of the column which he had decorated with Tritons; the half-man, half-fish servants of Neptune. The inscriptions give praise to the Vasa dynasty and list the names of the

column's creators.

Multiple restorations have helped the king's monument to survive. The figure was fortunate to survive a fall during the Second World War, with the king losing only a palm and his sword. The plinth and the column itself are now in their third incarnations. The original column was hewn of Polish marble; the second, made of pink Italian marble, lies on the lawn by the Royal Castle beside the East-West Route (*Trasa W-Z*).

Tunel na Trasie W-Z (The Tunnel under Castle Square)

The tunnel under Castle Square (*pl. Zamkowy*) was constructed in 1947-49. It provides a subterranean thoroughfare for the busy East-West Route (*Trasa W-Z*) and also a tramline which links the eastern part of the city with the western.

The Market Square of the Old Town is visited by numerous tourists

Escalators, installed by the entrance to the tunnel, link Castle Square to the East-West Route (*Trasa W-Z*) itself; their 'social-realistic' design resembles the Moscow or St Petersburg underground.

Most Gotycki (The Gothic Bridge)

This bridge marks the location of the former Cracow Gate (*Brama Krakowska*), which during medieval times, gave travellers access to the south. This two-span bridge was built on the cusp of the 15th and 16th centuries and is the Gate's sole surviving element, running over the moat to join with the foregate. It was discovered during restoration works in 1977 and is now partially reconstructed and was opened to pedestrians in 1983.

Horse-drawn carriage tours. The best way to sightsee the Old Town

Zamek Królewski (The Royal Castle)

(see p42-3)

Pałac Pod Blachą (The Palace under Metal Plate)

This palace adjoins the Royal Castle (*Zamek Królewski*), its name coming from the copper roofing which was an innovation in the 1720s. Originally, the building was a 17th-century townhouse, but Jerzy Dominik Lubomirski initiated its remodelling into the palace we see today. The palace was home to Prince Józef Poniatowski, a hero of the Napoleonic Wars, and his uncle, the last king of Poland, Stanislaus Augustus Poniatowski. Since 1932, the northern wing of the castle has hosted an exhibition of interior design.

In 1989, the palace was incorporated into the Royal Castle complex. Inside you'll find the world's largest collection of Caucasian fabrics – a unique part of a collection of eastern carpets gifted to the castle by Ms Teresa Sahakian. During the overhaul of the palace in 2004, archaeologists discovered the remains of an oval medieval burgh under the courtyard, which was more extensive than could have been expected.

Ulica Świętojańska (Świętojańska Street)

Świętojańska Street, leading from Castle Square to the Market Square of the Old Town, is lined with 15th-century townhouses. After the war they were reconstructed and their contemporary facades reflect their original 18th-century styling. No.8 is the St John the Baptist Cathedral (see Churches p62-7), No. 10 is the Holy Virgin Mary the Merciful Church (*Kościoły Matki Boskiej Łaskawej*), while

Houses on Szeroki Dunaj Street

No. 31 is the Townhouse under the Ship (*Kamienica Pod Okrętem*). The reconstruction of 1953 was overseen by Maciej Krasiński, who managed to retrieve a late-Renaissance portal and classically decorated facade with a relief of a ship. Świętojańska Street is a popular promenade abundant in souvenir shops and small eating establishments, and in summer with ice-cream stalls, candyfloss makers, orchestras and street artists to entertain passers-by.

Ulica Piwna (Piwna Street)

Piwna Street joins Castle Square with Szeroki Dunaj Street and is a favourite route of strolling Varsovians as well as tourists. Its nickname, 'Beer Street', has been in use since the 15th century but it previously bore others, such as 'Monk Street' or 'St Martin Street' due to the fact that in the 14th century the monastery complex of the Augustinian order was built here, together with St Martin's Church (*Kościoły św. Marcina*; see Churches p65).

In the past Piwna Street was inhabited by wealthy burgers, yet after the war it became a street of souvenir shops and restaurants. The facade of house No. 6 has a portal decorated with a pigeon motif. This motif dates from 1953, commemorating a protector of pigeons who lived in the ruins of the city after its liberation in 1945. House No. 18 was built in 1718 for the Crown Metricants: document keepers who worked in the royal archives and courts. It is decorated with a portal bearing an eagle and a keystone showing the date of its foundation.

Ulica Piekarska (Piekarska Street)

Piekarska Street links Podwale Street with Piwna Street, which later widens into Zapiecek Square adjoining the Market Square of the Old Town. The name *Piekarska* (baker) comes from the bakers and millers who lived in its once timber, now brick houses. At the confluence of Piekarska Street and Rycerska Street a small square called the Inferno (*Piekiełko*) once existed. Witches were burned at the stake here in the 16th and 17th centuries. It is also the place where the unsuccessful assassin of King Sigismund III Vasa, Michał Piekarski, was executed. Under interrogation he was tortured and spoke senselessly on various subjects, giving rise to the Polish saying 'You're blathering like Piekarski being tortured.'

The Townhouse under the Peacock (*Kamienica pod Pawiem*) at No. 4 is also worth seeing. It was built in the 1750s and designed by Antonio Fontana, to be reconstructed between 1959-61 and the decoration of the classical facade preserved. A monument to Jan Kiliński stands at the junction of Piekarska and Podwale Streets.

Pomnik Jana Kilińskiego (Monument to Jan Kilińsk)

This monument, sculpted by Stanisław Jackowski, was unveiled in 1935 and positioned on Krasiński Square (*Plac Krasińskich*). During the German occupation it was removed and partially damaged, to be placed in a new location on 3rd May Avenue (*al. 3 Maja*). Its present location on Podwale Street was chosen in 1959. The monument shows the shoemaker Jan Kiliński, a leader of the Old Town's inhabitants during the Kościuszko Uprising, who overran the seat of the Russian tsar's ambassador. Kiliński was promoted by General Tadeusz Kościuszko to the rank of colonel of the Polish Army.

Kanonia (Cathedral Chapter Square)

This small triangular square behind the cathedral is the site of the former cemetery, which existed there until 1880. The sole relic of the cemetery is a rococo statue of The Mother of

---

Sigismund III Vasa

Sigismund III Vasa (1566-1632), the son of Swedish King Johan III Vasa and the Polish princess Anna Jagiellonka, was king of Poland from 1587, and from 1592-98 king of Sweden too - his desire for the Swedish throne bringing about the long-lasting Polish-Swedish wars of 1563-1721. He oversaw the gradual transfer of the capital from Krakow to Warsaw and in 1598 he initiated the remodelling of the local castle into both the royal seat and the seat of the Senate, the latter being specifically the castle's Senate Hall (*Sala Senatu*). Next, he began the development of the royal residence from the Vistula river side of the city. The whole royal court finally moved to the Royal Castle in Warsaw in 1611. The castle had been extended between 1601-03 and was extended again between 1610-19 to become a two-storey building standing around a pentagon. Sigismund III Vasa was also a patron of the arts and a connoisseur of music; this patronage played a vital role in the early development of Polish baroque.

God, dated 1771. The houses of the Curia and Cathedral Chapter surrounding the square were reconstructed after the Second World War. The house numbered 20/22 is the narrowest in Warsaw and above its entrance there are only two windows on each floor.

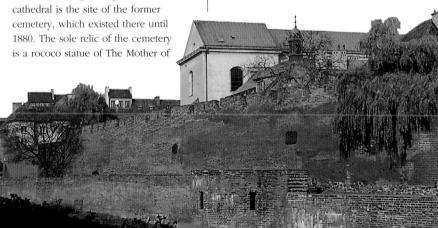

Cathedral Chapter Square also possesses a bell, cast by the court bell-maker of Ladislas IV Vasa, Daniel Tym, who produced the bronze statue of King Sigismund III Vasa which crowns the Column on Castle Square. The bell was commissioned for the Jesuit Church in Jarosław, but before 1939 was placed in Warsaw's National Museum and since 1972 has been located in its present home.

Rynek Starego Miasta (The Old Town Market Square)

A rectangular square of 90m by 73m has existed on the site of the modern Market Square since the turn of the 13th and 14th centuries, and until the 19th century it was the focal point of the local economy and municipal administration. The Market Square was the site of a variety of festivals, local trade fairs and sometimes even executions of criminals. Between 1429 and 1817 it possessed a high-towered City Hall surrounded by townhouses. It was from this Square that on 2nd December 1789 a procession of burghers dressed in black and led by the mayor of Warsaw, Jan Dekiert, petitioned the king and the Diet for civil rights. Today, the Market Square is a place to find orchestras, street artists and the music of Warsaw's sole barrel organ player who performs together with his parrot! In summer the Market is full of outdoor cafés with colourful umbrellas.

Wąski i Szeroki Dunaj (The Narrow and Wide Dunaj)

The name 'Dunaj' originates from the local stream, which runs away from the area. Wąski (narrow) Dunaj joins the Market Square with area of the defensive walls, while Szeroki (wide) Dunaj is a square adjacent to it. The streets here were laid out at the turn of the 14th century. In medieval times the houses standing here belonged to the Jewish community and when their timber houses burned down in 1478, new brick houses were built. House No.10 was built in the 17th century and hosted the Guild of Shoemakers. It was reconstructed in the years 1949-53 and received new sgraffito decoration, and is now the home of the Leather Handicrafts Guild.

In the 17th century Szeroki Dunaj Square was a fish market, later to become a flower and vegetable market. Butchers' stalls

The view of Market Square from Świętojańska Street

existed at one time too and a reminder of which is the Butchers' Gate, built around 1632. House No. 13, is the seat of the Guild of Miscellaneous Crafts, while house No. 5 was home to the shoemaker Jan Kiliński, who helped lead the Kościuszko Uprising.

Mury Miejskie (Defensive Walls) and Pomnik Małego Powstańca (Monument to the Little Insurgent)

Warsaw's Old Town is ringed by sections of age-old defensive walls. Walks along these walls are possible along a trail running between the inner and outer lines. The remains of the eighth keep (tower) in the outer circle of walls are home to the monument to the Little Insurgent (*Pomnik Małego Powstańca*) cast by Jerzy Jarmuszewski. The monument, symbolising the young people who fought during the 1944 Warsaw Uprising, depicts a boy with a machine gun in hand and a helmet which is too large for him. To reach the Barbican, follow the course of the walls.

Barbakan (The Barbican)

The Barbican, built in 1548 by the Venetian Giovanni Battista, was an important element of the defensive walls, extended by the inhabitants of Warsaw between the first half of the 14th century and the 1550s. Entry to Warsaw was gained by one of two gates, the Krakow Gate (*Brama Krakowska*) to the south and the New Town Gate (*Brama Nowomiejska*) to the north, or by way of the Barbican. The Krackow Gate no longer exists in its entirety, its only remaining element being the Gothic bridge (see p33).

The Barbican, fully restored by 1954

The Barbican is a round construction, reinforced with four defensive towers, which was partially demolished and subsequently built back up in the 18th and 19th centuries. In the years 1936-38 its remains were excavated and the lower sections have since been reconstructed together with part of the walls and neighbouring Gunpower Keep.

The Barbican and its defensive walls are a meeting place for artists selling their works. Recently it has been a stage for a fortune teller, musical ensembles and mime artists such as an executioner frightening passers-by with an adze (a tool used in wood carving).

The Barbican's walls impress from all angles

Walk: Old Town Market Square

Start at Zapiecek Square, which opens onto the Old Town Market Square, pass the Varsovian Mermaid monument and stop off at the Warsaw Historical Museum and the Adam Mickiewicz Museum of Literature before crossing Stone Stair Street to finish at the viewing platform on Dung Hill. *Allow: about 2 hours.*

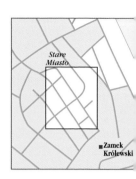

1 Zapiecek Square

After the Second World War the Zapiecek Gallery, a famed and ebullient gallery of contemporary art with numerous exhibitions, was established here. In 1985 a plaque commemorating the enrolment of the Old Town Market Square on the UNESCO World Heritage List was embedded in the pavement.

2 Pomnik Syrenki (The Mermaid Monument)

The legendary Mermaid monument stands

Warsaw Mermaid - the symbol of the city

in the centre of the Market Square. The figure, half-woman half-fish, became the official symbol of the city in 1938.

3 The Warsaw Historical Museum

Warsaw's Historical Museum is to be found within eleven townhouses in the Old Town and in three houses on Nowomiejska Street. The history of Warsaw is presented in paintings, drawings, graphics, maps, carvings, photographs, handicrafts and in the belongings of famous Varsovians. The city's reconstruction is shown in a film, while architectural ornamentation discovered after the war in the ruins of the Old Town is exhibited in the *lapidarium* in the yard.

4 ul. Kamienne Schodki (Stone Stair Street)

This picturesque little street of steps provides a passage from Krzywe Koło Street near the Market Square to Brzozowa Street and later Bugaj Street. It is popular with photographers and painters who come to capture its appearance.

5 The Adam Mickiewicz Museum of Literature

Located in the 15th-century Orlemusowska and Balcerowska Townhouses (Nos. 18 and 20), it documents the works of the Polish national poet Adam Mickiewicz. Manuscripts, personal effects and first editions are held across ten rooms. There are also personal effects, manuscripts, recordings and original furnishings from the studios of other great Polish writers including Julian Tuwim and Leopold Staff.

6 Gnojna Góra (Dung Hill)

Celna Street has a viewing platform, which offers a panorama of the Vistula River and the right bank of the city. The name is not accidental! It has its origin in the piles of waste removed from the Old

Stone Stair Street

Town in medieval times, this area having been the very first rubbish dump.

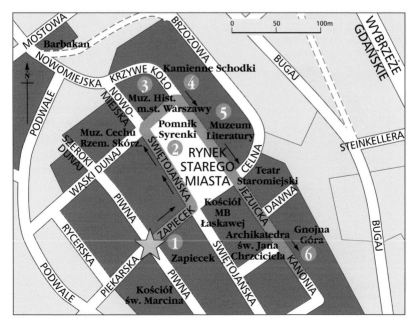

Located in the heart of Warsaw, the Old Town Market Square became an unusual open-air gallery. The townhouses surrounding the square on four sides were rebuilt following wartime damage, each with its own name. In addition, each side of the Market Square is named after 18th-century Diet *(Sejm)* activists: merchant Jan Dekert, lawyer Franiszek Barss, statesman and scholar Hugo Kołłątaj and the first mayor of Warsaw, Ignacy Zakrzewski-Wyssogota.

On the northern 'Jam Dekert' side, the late-Renaissance Baryczkowska Townhouse (No.32) has Gothic vaulting

built at the turn of the 14th and 15th centuries, ground floor furnishings, an attic and a portal bearing the mason's mark of the Baryczko family; it was remodelled for the family in 1616-33. The early-baroque Falkiewicz Townhouse (No.28) is crowned with an attic decorated on both sides with carvings of the Holy Mother of God, St Stanislaus and St Elizabeth.

The eastern Franiszek Barss side is adorned with dormer windows and rooftop lanterns, which formerly served to illuminate the staircases. The Orlemusowska Townhouse at No.18, with its beautiful facade and preserved baroque portal, and the Balcerowska Townhouse at No.20, with a fragment of Gothic portal, reconstructed Gothic vestibule and relics of old polychrome paintings, harbour the Adam Mickiewicz Museum of Literature (see p39). The 15th Giza Townhouse at No.6 has a preserved 17th-century portal and takes its name from the Giza family. It was reconstructed after the war with the restoration of old classical decoration.

The western Hugo Kołłątaj side includes the Fukier Townhouse (No.27) with its painted Sluck belt, an item worn by a Polish nobleman dressed in the national costume, *kontusz*. This 15th-century townhouse was the property of the Korba family which ran a winery here in the 16th century, one famed for its perfect old Polish mead *(miód pitny)* and Hungarian wine. In 1810 the building became the property of the

Fukiers. Its appearance is a result of reconstruction and restoration of the classical elements created in 1782. The townhouse belongs to the Art Historian's Society, the cellars hosting an excellent restaurant managed by the Gessler family, which continues the traditions of the Fukiers.

The 15th-century Townhouse under St Anna at No.31 *(Kamienica Pod św. Anną)* takes its name from the statue of the saint decorating a small corner niche. Its Gothic wall with arched niches on the Wąski Dunaj Street side survived multiple remodellings and the war, and in 1913-15, during restoration work led by Władysław Marconi and Władysław Wojciechowski, Gothic elements were discovered. In 1913 it was designated as the seat of the History Lovers' Society; after wartime damage it was reconstructed in the years 1948-53 to become the seat of the Polish History Institute of the Polish Academy of Science, and of the Polish Historical Society.

On the southern 'Zakrzewski' side of the square, the Townhouse under the Lion on the corner (No.13) is decorated with a rococo relief of a lion and a partially preserved painting showing the famous painter Zofia Stryjeńska in the 1920s. The wall on the Świętojańska Street side supports a sun clock designed by the clock collector Tadeusz Przypkowski. The Townhouse under the Basilisk *(Kamienica Pod Bazyliszkiem)* at No.5, with its classically decorated facade and reconstructed medallion, serves as a restaurant. The Golden Townhouse *(Kamienica Złocista)* at No.7 is ornamented with late-Renaissance decorations and a grid with the initials SB, standing for Stanisław Baryczka, the former owner.

Left: 17th century portal of Baryczkowska Townhouse
Upper right: houses on the Barss' side
Right central: the head of a man decorates the Townhouse under the Little Black Boy

The Royal Castle

The Royal Castle (*Zamek Królewski*) was reconstructed thanks to the efforts of the whole community in the years 1971-88 and was subsequently enrolled on the UNESCO World Heritage List together with the Old Town complex. The reconstruction of the royal residence generated real enthusiasm, with special committees being spontaneously established both in Poland and abroad. The castle was gifted precious items, such as several works from King Stanislaus Augustus Poniatowski's collection, including two paintings by Rembrandt.

Sigismunt III Vasa's Tower crowns the castle

In August 1569 the Polish-Lithuanian Diet chose Warsaw to be the site of its convocations and of free royal elections. It was now that the intensive development of the castle began, to suit the needs of the king and Diet. All kings from Sigismund II Augustus to Stefan Bathory with his wife Anna Jagiellonka visited the castle to ensure the support of the Parliament.

Once Sigismund III Vasa took the decision to move the capital from Krakow to Warsaw, a brick castle was built on the site of the previous castle of the Dukes of Mazovia. The Italian architects Giovanni

The Facade of the Palace under the Metal Plate

Trevano, Giacomo Rodondo and Matteo Castelli built the early-baroque, two-storey pentagonal castle between 1598 and 1619. To the buildings of the original castle were added the Grand Court (*Dwór Wielki*), Minor Court (*Dwór Mniejszy*), Grodzka Tower (*Wieża Grodzka*) and New House of Sigismund II Augustus (*Dom Nowy Zygmunta Augusta*).

The castle was later extended many times. During the kingship of August III Wettin, the 'Wettin wing' was added to the Vistula River side. It received a late-baroque elevation decorated with carvings by Jan Jerzy Plerch. In the time of Stanislaus Augustus Poniatowski, the Royal Library was built according to the design of Domenico Merlini, abutting the Palace under Metal Plate (see p33). Until 1795, when Poland finally disappeared from the map in the Third Partition, the palace was the royal seat, and included a hall for deputies. The castle was the home of Diet proceedings and it was here that the Constitution of 3rd May was passed. The second of the added wings, the *Bacciarellówka*, was named after the

Italian painter Marcello Bacciarelli, who managed the *Malarnia* School of Painting. Between 1818-21 a classical viewing terrace was added, supported by arcades and designed by Jakub Kubicki. Below spread the royal gardens, which are currently being reconstructed.

The castle was burned down by the German army in 1939 and blown up in 1944. The reconstructed building, completed in 1988, recalls the residence as it was in the first half of the

Richly decorated Marble Cabinet with the imposing plafond.

18th century when the facade on the Vistula side was remodelled in the rococo style; the interior furnishings are largely original. Thankfully, during the evacuation of the castle in 1944, employees of the National Museum managed to save some furniture, carvings, paintings and elements of the woodwork and wainscoting.

The Gothic history of the castle is recalled by the vaulting of the cellars. A feature of the first floor well worth seeing is the famous Canaletto Hall, which holds paintings of 18th-century views by Bernardo Bellotto, also known as Canaletto. The most attractive hall is the Great Hall, or Ballroom, with its 17 gilded columns and the largest Polish *plafond* with motifs from mythology. In the Halls of the Diet and Senate, paintings by Jan

Matejko were hung, one among them the famous depiction of the Constitution of 3rd May. In rooms on the second floor, the studio of the famous Polish writer Stefan Żeromski has been reconstructed, together with the office of the very first Polish President Gabriel Narutowicz and the Hall of the Polish Government-in-Exile.

The breathtaking Marble Room was the location of the famous Thursday Dinners when King Stanislaus Augustus Poniatowski met with leading lights of the Enlightenment. The room is decorated with multicoloured marbles and portraits of the Polish kings painted by Marcello Bacciarelli and Jan Bogumił Plersch. The new *plafond* is a recreation of the original work by two artists, Stefan Garwatowski and Jan Karczewski.

The New Town

The New Town (*Nowe Miasto*), like the Old, is one of the quarters of the capital most frequently visited by both Varsovians and visitors alike. Its unique character is a result of the reconstruction of the townhouses on the New Town Market Square and on Freta, Kościelna, Mostowa and Świętojerska Streets, together with the beauty of the quarter's palaces and churches. The area abounds in statues, while its buildings house restaurants, cafés, shops and galleries.

The Baroque facade of the Sapieha's Palace

The New Town was built at the turn of the 14th and 15th centuries along the route leading from the oldest part of the city to the town of Zakroczym on the Vistula River, commemorated in the naming of Zakroczymska Street. In contrast to the old Warsaw, the new Warsaw was a place settled by craftsmen and it never possessed defensive walls. At the outset timber houses were built, but these were replaced by brick versions in the 18th and early 19th centuries. In 1792, the New Town lost its individuality and was incorporated into a united urban complex. It was 80 percent damaged during the Second World War and reconstructed in the 1950s, its architecture now relating to the style of the turn of the 18th and 19th centuries.

The Smallest House in Warsaw

The Church of the Holy Ghost (*Kościół św.Ducha; see Churches p64*) is adjacent to the smallest building in Warsaw. Now a kiosk selling newspapers, this tiny classical house was built in the late 18th century on the very smallest available plot, one of

only a few square metres in size.
Address: *Długa 1 Street*

Raczyński Palace and Archiwum Główna Akt Dawnych (The Main Document Archive)

Constructed in the years 1702-04 as a regular house, this building was remodelled into a palace at some time around the 1750s. The next period of remodelling was performed for Marshal Kazimierz Raczyński by the royal architect J C Kamsetzer in 1786, when the ballroom located on the first floor was decorated with stucco works and paintings. In the 19th century it became the seat of the Governmental Commission of Justice, later the Ministry of Justice in the interwar period (1918-1939). The palace was damaged during the Warsaw Uprising and Nazis murdered wounded rebels here.

The palace was reconstructed in 1948-50 in the classical style to become a square three-storey palace with a portico supported by four Ionian columns. It is currently home to the Main Document Archive.
Address: *Długa 7 Street*

Ulica Mostowa (Mostowa Street)

Originally, Mostowa Street was simply a road passing through a stream-riven gorge to the ford of the Vistula. When the permanent bridge over Vistula was built in 1568-75 the street gained the name of Bridge Street, or *ulica Mostowa* in Polish. In 1595 the street was paved and later, in the 18th century, was built up with classical brick houses, the homes of craftsmen, tradesmen, court clerks and wardens at the prison in Bridge Gate (*Brama Mostowa*, now a theatre). The street became famous for its eating houses and illegal drinking dens. After being rebuilt following the Second World War, this street running down to the river became a popular cul-de-sac, frequently painted and photographed.

Stara Prochownia (The Old Gunpowder Store)

In 1581 the Bridge Gate (*Brama Mostowa*) was built to protect the bridge over Vistula that had been constructed in 1560-73 (the bridge was damaged by flood in 1603). In 1646 the gate was remodelled as a gunpowder storeroom, and during the Kościuszko Uprising in 1794 turned into a prison for traitors. After 1831, the prison was closed and the gate changed into a tenement which was burned during the Warsaw Uprising and reconstructed in 1961-65. The Old Gunpowder Store currently hosts the theatre *Stara Prochownia*.
Address: Rybaki 2

Rynek Nowego Miasta (The New Town Market Square)

In the past this square was an integral part of the new Warsaw, a spacious, rectangular square laid out at the turn of the 14th and 15th centuries, which, until 1818, possessed its own city hall. The square, however, was diminished owing to unplanned construction work and in fact now resembles a triangle. After suffering damage in 1944, the square's houses were rebuilt in the 1950s, together

The Warsaw Uprising monument on the Krasińskich Square; in the background the seat of the courts.

with the church and convent of the Benedictines of the Perpetual Adoration of the Blessed Sacrament (*Kościół Sakramentek*), which stand on the eastern side of the square. The new architecture is close in character to that of the turn of the 18th and 19th centuries; the elevations are decorated with social realistic polychromatic paintings and sgraffito. The Market Square possesses a 19th-century iron well on the Freta Street side bearing the New Town coat of arms of the unicorn and virgin.

Pałac Sapiehów (Sapieha Palace)

This palace was built by the Chancellor of the Great Lithuanian County, Jan Fryderyk Sapieha, between 1731 and 1746 according to the plans of J Z Deybel. It is a late-baroque construction of two wings with rococo elevations and rich sculptural decoration; the courtyard was previously sealed with a gate. In the early 19th century an outbuilding was added, which became a barracks for the 4th Infantry Regiment, a regiment to gain fame in the period of the November Uprising and later Polish-Russian War (1830-31). The palace burned down in 1944, yet was rebuilt to serve as a school building.
Address: Zakroczymska 6

Romuald Traugutt Park

Romuald Traugutt Park was laid out in the area of the former fortress and Citadel (*Cytadela*) in 1925 in accordance with the plans of Leon Danielewicz and Stanisław Życieński-Zadora. The park and gardens commemorate Romuald Traugutt, the leader of the January Uprising who was shot in 1864 at Legions Fort (*Fort Legionów*) together with the members of the Temporary National Government. Of particular interest for visitors to this well-located and well-kept park, is the sculpture *Motherhood* (*Macierzyństwo*) created by Wacław Szymanowski, the

The Monument to the Dead and the Killed on the East

very same sculptor who designed the monument to Fryderyk Chopin in Łazienki park.
Address: Zakroczymska Street

Zdrój Królewski (The Royal Spring)

The neoclassical building standing close to the Citadel (*Cytadela*) is the enclosure protecting this spring, famous for its appetising waters. It was built in the early 18th century and subsequently remodelled in 1771 at the command of King Stanislaus Augustus Poniatowski. It was buried during the construction of the Citadel in 1832, but uncovered a few years later and reconstructed. Enrico Marconi is responsible for its present appearance.

The Execution Gate of the Warsaw Citadel

Cydadela Warszawska (The Warsaw Citadel)

Following suppression of the November Uprising in 1831, the Russian Army reinforced Warsaw's existing fortifications, between the 1880s and the Great War, encasing Warsaw in forts of earth and brick. The Citadel itself was not only a fortress but a prison which terrified the political opponents of the despotic Russian tsar Nicholas I. Pavilion No.10 was the high security wing where patriotic Polish activists were confined, among them the priest Piotr Ściegienny, the insurrectionist Romuald Traugutt, the politician Roman Dmowski and the warrior Józef Piłsudski, who fortunately escaped from a transport to Siberia and later became marshal. In a completely different category of prisoner were the communist revolutionaries Feliks Dzierżyński and Julian Marchlewski.

Until 1939 the fortifications were an important element of the city's defence, but today the Citadel hosts the European Academy of Art and the Museum of Independence (*Muzeum Niepodległości*). One of the museum's exhibits is a Russian horse-drawn vehicle on wheels or runners called a *kibitka*, which was used to transport Polish political leaders and their supporters deep into Siberia. The fortress towers over Vistula hill are surrounded by a moat and wall, four classical gates providing access.

Walk: New Town Market Square

This is a popular trail will both Varsovians and tourists. Walkers begin at the Barbican (*Barbakan*) and by way of Freta Street make their way to the New Town Market Square. The square may be circumvented via Freta, Kościelna, Przyrynek or Piesza Streets. Walkers are made welcome at cafés and restaurants en route, their owners setting up tables outside in summer.

Allow 1 hour.

1 Freta Street

The name *Freta* is probably derived from the German word *Freiheit*, or free trade. The even-numbered side of Freta Street is dominated by the Dominican Church, St Jack's Church and the biographical Maria Skłodowska-Curie Museum. Almost opposite the museum, on the odd-numbered side of the street is the Museum of Asia and the Pacific together with the Asian Gallery. The street is also filled with antique shops, restaurants and cafés.

St Jack's Church dominates Freta Street

Market Square in the New Town

2 The Marie Curie Museum

Located in the house where Maria Skłodowska-Curie, the first double Nobel prize-winning woman-scientist, was born, this museum exhibits furniture, photos, family souvenirs, documents and several measuring devices from her husband, Pierre Curie's, laboratory. The items of greatest value are the photographs showing Maria, who began the history of radioactivity and discovered polonium and radium, giving lectures and working at the laboratory. She is also seen with the illustrious scientist Albert Einstein.

3 Kościół św. Franciszka, Serafickiego (St Francis Seraph Church)

The first Holy Mass following the liberation of Warsaw in 1945 took place in this church on the corner of Zakroczymska and Franciszkańska Streets. For connoisseurs of music, the highlight must surely be the incredible sound of the organ. The chapel on the left is the eternal resting place of the remains of St Vitalis, who lies in a glass coffin, the relics gifted by Pope Benedict XIV in 1754.

4 Kościół św. Benona (St Benno of Meissen Church)

Built after 1643 as a timber church for St Benno's Brotherhood, the wooden building was destroyed by fire and from 1740-44 reconstructed in brick together with a monastery. In 1787 King Stanislaus Augustus Poniatowski gifted the complex to the Redemptorists, who set up two orphanages. In 1808 the building was turned into a factory producing knives and other utensils, but it was razed in 1944 only to be reconstructed by the Redemptorists. It received a baroque facade and modern interior furnishings, a contrast with the old statues.
Address: Piesza 1

5 Kościół św. Kazimierza i klasztor Sakramentek

(St Casimir's Church and the Convent of the Benedictines of the Perpetual Adoration of the Blessed Sacrament)

This complex of church and convent built in the years 1668-1692 was founded by Queen Marie Casimire d'Arquien Sobieska and her husband. The complex possesses pieces of baroque art and the gravestone of Marie Charlotte de Bouillon, who was the granddaughter of Marie's husband. The gravestone is decorated with a shield and falling crown symbolising the death of the last representative of the royal family. The terraced garden at the back of the convent, which runs down to the Vistula, survived the war.

During Mass the Gregorian Choral is sung and on the second Sunday of every month Mass is said in Latin.

In the 17th century, the Royal Castle was remodelled in both Renaissance and baroque style by King Sigismund III Vasa and his sons. Kazimierzowski Palace, was also remodelled and is now the seat of Warsaw University.

King Sigismund III Vasa was patron of the arts and a connoisseur, whose sons, King Ladislas IV Vasa *(Władysław IV)* and Johan II Casimir Vasa *(Jan Kazimierz)*, both continued his work. In the halls of the Royal Castle paintings by Rubens and Rembrandt were hung, while the court employed Italian architects including the Manierist Santi Gucci and, fans of the baroque, Trevano and Locci. Visitors to the National Museum should also take a look at the painting of the Silesian baroque master, Michael Willmann.

In the time of Ladislas IV Vasa, the leading architect in Warsaw was the Dutch Tylman van Gameren, who had arrived in the city in 1660 to take up the post of military engineer at the court of Marshal Lubomirski. It was not long before he was recognised as an excellent and imaginative architect and he eventually came to be ennobled by the Polish Diet. His most famous secular building is the Krasiński Palace on Krasiński Square with its rich sculptural decoration. Among Tylman's sacral buildings are the Bernardine Church in the Czerniaków quarter and St Casimir's Church and the Convent of the Benedictines of the Perpetual Adoration of the Blessed Sacrament in the Nowe Miasto quarter.

Also in the baroque style is the Tomb of the Unknown Soldier, which now stands in a place previously chosen by King August II Wettin, at the beginning of Warsaw's urban unification, for the construction of the huge Saski Palace.

The elegant rococo Church of the Sisters of the Marian Visitation in Krakowskie Przedmieście Street was the creation of another team of architects; this perfectly composed church was founded by Marie Louise Gonzaga de Nevers, Queen of Poland and wife first of Ladislas IV Vasa. This religious queen

Józef Poniatowski organised exuberant balls, while the baroque palace of the Sobieskis in Wilanów is a pleasure for the eyes with its architecture, interiors and stylish gardens. On Senatorska Street, the Primate's Palace with its gardens and cellars now serves as a Conference and Exhibition Centre.

Plenty of residences built in the Renaissance style and damaged in the 17th-century Polish-Swedish Wars were reconstructed in the baroque. The largest number of such remodelled residences is located between Krakowskie Przedmieście Street, Teatralny Square (*Plac Teatralny*) and Krasiński Square (*Plac Krasińskich*). Today these buildings serve a public purpose, as ministries, offices or university buildings, and give this part of Warsaw its elegant character.

also founded the two St Casimir orphanages on Tamka Street.

Another church representative of the baroque is located far away from the city centre in the Ursynów quarter. St Catherine's Church was remodelled from the Gothic in 1742-45 and is claimed to be the oldest parish of Warsaw's left bank.

The baroque as distinct from the Renaissance quickly found for itself a place in the Mazovia region and remained for a considerable time. It suited a nobleman's aspirations; in the baroque Palace under Metal Plate, Prince

Left: The facade of the Kraśińskis Square
Upper right: The baroque interior of the Church of Sisters of the Visitation of Mary
Bottom right: The interior with baroque furnishings of the Wilanów Palace

Around Teatralny Square

The cultural heart of Warsaw is Plac Teatralny, or in English Theatre Square, which is to be found close to the Old Town and Krakowskie Przedmieście Street. Historically, the square's functions differed, yet it was always important to the life of the city. In the 17th century, Queen Marie Casimire d'Arquien Sobieska initiated the construction of the wide-roofed shopping complex named Marieville, or *Marywil* in Polish.

One of the sculptures in the Saski Garden

The administrative centre of the capital moved to Theatre Square at the beginning of the 19th century when the old town hall was abandoned, the municipal authority re-purchasing the 18th-century Jabłonowski Palace (*Pałac Jabłonowskich*) and designating it their new seat. The palace served this purpose until it burned down, whereafter it was reconstructed as a banking centre (see The City's Modern Architecture, p60-1). The present home of the authority is the truly modern building closing the square from the north, which was constructed just a few years ago. Its facade makes references to the earlier seat of Warsaw's local government.

In the 19th century the square was dominated by the huge National Theatre (*Teatr Narodowy*). However, with the connections of the Polish capital to literary history being as interesting as they are, Warsaw had understandable frustration in waiting for a true theatre such as this for as long as it had to.

For example, there are a number of events in the lives of the Dukes of Mazovia, which could have provided

inspiration for Shakespeare's *A Winter's Tale*. Some believe that the play may have being based on the story of a poor dutchess, Ludmiła, who was killed by her husband, Siemowit III of Mazovia, in the castle in the village of Rawa Mazowiecka. Siemowit III believed that his wife had been unfaithful and was carrying the child of a peasant from the village. As such, after she had given birth to the baby boy, Siemowit killed her and the baby was given to a poor woman. After many years Ludmiła's sister, the Dutchess Małgorzata, found the boy and brought him before Siemowit. The resemblance of the one to the other was so strong that Siemowit could have no doubts as to his being the father. This tragic story may well have been carried back to England by John Green's theatre troupe. Green being one of Shakespeare's actors who visited Warsaw in 1616-17 to stage the bard's plays at the court of Sigismund III Vasa.

Another Polish connection to Shakespeare involves the play *Richard II*: Richard II Plantagenet's wife, Anna of Bohemia, was a daughter of Elizabeth of

Pomerania, who had her origins in the Polish village of Słupsk.

Ladislaus IV Vasa (*Władysław IV*) had organised the first permanent theatre, but he preferred Italian artists and Italian opera, as did August II Wettin (*August II Mocny*). The father of Polish theatre is seen to be Wojciech Bogusławski, an actor, director, writer and freemason. In 1781 he managed the first actors' partnership, which popularised the national repertoire, although unfortunately the partnership was to be bankrupted; patronage of public theatre was then taken over by the last Polish king, Stanislaus Augustus Poniatowski. A monument to Wojciech Bogusławski stands in front of the Great Theatre (*Teatr Wielki*), which did not exist in his day, the building having been designed by Antonio Corazzi in 1825 and finished 18 years later. Then, the repertoire was subject to the Russian tsar's censorship, which is why it could be neither national nor up-to-date. A great cultural event was the premiere of the opera Halka by Stanisław Moniuszko in January 1858, the composer moving to Warsaw to take up the position of conductor. Moniuszko also composed another national opera, *The Haunted Manor* (*Straszny Dwór*). His monument stands on the Teatralny Square. One more great artist must be mentioned in this regard, one who despite never having been to Warsaw is regarded as the creator of the Polish national scene: Adam Mickiewicz, the

Polish national poet. His monument stands on Krakowskie Przedmieście Street.

Mickiewicz had the power to cause both reverie and reaction. In March 1968, communist censors ordered the removal of posters for his *Forefathers Eve* (*Dziady*), as audiences were reacting to every anti-Russian suggestion in the text and actors performing in a seeming trance. In response, students flocked to the Mickiewicz monument and street fighting broke out; students, political opponents and intellectuals were to face the violence and anti-Semitic attacks of the communist government. This was no longer just fiction; this was for real.

The theatre building has caught fire on several occasions, yet the worst damage occurred during the Warsaw Uprising. Subsequent reconstruction lasted for 20 years, as phase after phase was completed, with the theatre finally reopened in 1965. The building occupies the whole southern side of Teatralny Square. Visitors may admire the classical facade with its elongated cornices, which

Classical building on Bankowy Square – seat of municipal authority

The relics of the colonnade of the Saski Palace, today the Grave of the Unknown Soldier

sharpen the line of the side wings, its colonnade on the ground floor and its antique sculptures. The central part of the building is decorated with a huge portico, above which two artists, Adam Myjak and Antoni Pastwa, placed the Triumphal Quadrig, which weighs around five tons. The first architect, Antonio Corazzi, had planned the Quadriga, yet the political storms of the November Uprising prevented him completing his work. His design had to wait for around 170 years for its realisation, until the time of Poland's full sovereignty. The building not only holds the National Theatre (*Teatr Narodowy*), but also the National Opera (*Opera Narodowa*) and the Museum of Theatre (*Muzeum Teatru*), all of which employ the very best artists.

The rear of the building has been reconstructed and is less decorative than before. It is also screened by an office block designed by Sir Norman Foster,

which stands on Piłsudskiego Square (*Plac Piłsudskiego*). One of the streets running from the square is Bielańska Street, which intersects Daniłłowiczowska Street with its House under the Kings (*Dom pod Królami*). This building is particularly eye-catching for a frieze bearing the busts of Polish kings which runs between the ground and first floors. It is not known when or by whom this 'royal gallery', ending on Sigismund III Vasa, was sculpted, although the next group of kings, including Stanislaus Augustus Poniatowski, was added during reconstruction in the 19th century. Wierzbowa Street ends at Teatralny Square with the classical Petrykus house and its eating establishments.

The present Piłsudskiego Square (*Plac Piłsudskiego*) was created when King August II Wettin ordered the razing of the area between what is today's Żelazna Street and Krakowskie Przedmieście Street (approximately 1.5km of buildings in linear distance), in order to build the tremendous Saski Palace (*Pałac Saski*). The body and wings of this palace occupied the entire square; one of the two streets coming out of it ran to Mirowskie Barracks, the second to Trzech Krzyży Square. The project was supervised by a team of architects under the guidance of K F Pöppleman. The palace gardens and gates were later to be levelled by Great Prince Constantin, the Russian governor and brother of the tsar, so as to make space for military training and parades, his beloved entertainment. The central part of the palace was also to be destroyed to make way for the Sobor Orthodox Church, complete with a 70m-high tower. When Poland won its independence, the Sobor was removed. In 1854 the most modern and elegant of Warsaw's hotels, the Europejski, appeared on the limits of the square.

After the Warsaw Uprising all of the buildings in Saski Square had gone, only part of a colonnade surviving, which now serves as the Tomb of the Unknown Soldier (*Grób Nieznanego Żołnierza*), whose

relics were brought from the battlefield of Lviv in 1925. The square also provides space for a monument to Marshal Piłsudski, who looks upon the tomb while resting on his sabre. The tomb is guarded by soldiers of the Polish Army and is where official delegations come to lay wreaths. The Saski Gardens (*Ogród Saski*) with its elegant fountains also survived and is open to the public.

After the Second World War the square was renamed Victory Square (*Plac Zwycięstwa*) and the Victoria Hotel was built, a functional construction lacking aesthetic loftiness. On Małachowskiego Square (*Plac Małachowskiego*), not far from the gardens, is the Zachęta National Gallery of Art; its building was designed by Stefan Szyller and is richly decorated with a facade presenting a variety artists of various eras at work, as well as a symbolic scene with lions, muses and genius. Inside, the gallery offers exhibitions of painting, sculpture and photography. Zachęta Gallery was witness to

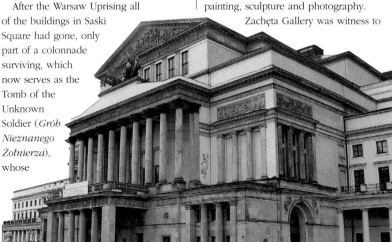

The National Theatre

Houses on Miodowa Street

the tragic death of the first Polish President, Gabriel Narutowicz, who was assassinated by Eligiusz Niewiadomski.

To the north-west of Teatralny Square is Krasiński Square (*Plac Krasińskich*). This is occupied by the capital's most remarkable secular building, the Palace of the Republic (*Pałac Rzeczpospolitej*), built by Tylman van Gameren for the royal court clerk Jan Dobrogost Krasiński in 1677-83. The carvings in the central projection refer to Marek Waleriusz Krasiński, the legendary founder of the family, who apparently was once assisted by a crow during a duel. Above the main portal on the second floor is a cartouche bearing the coat of arms of Poland.

The palace was private property until 1765 when it was bought by the National Treasury Office to host a number of different institutions. After a fire in 1782 it was remodelled by J Fontana and D Merlini, and the palace with its stucco decoration now houses the old documents and special collections of the National Library (*Biblioteka Narodowa*). At the rear is a park and former garden.

A branch of Krasiński Square is named Miodowa Street and this is perpendicular to Senatorska Street, which joins four squares: Zamkowy, Teatralny, Piłsudskiego and Bankowy. Yet there is also another small square on Senatorska Street itself, on which the Primate's Palace (*Pałac Prymasowski*) is situated. In the past the position of Primate, the highest in the Polish Catholic Church, was reserved for archbishops of Gniezno whose home this palace was. It is another of Tylman van Gameren's works.

Crossing Teatralny Square westwards, Senatorska leads on to the next notable square, Bankowy. Neo-Renaissance buildings designed by Corazzi line the western frontage, one of them the 18th-century Mostowski Palace (*Pałac Mostowskich*), which Corazzi rebuilt for the Home Affairs Commission and is now the headquarters of the metropolitan police. Post-war buildings are easily recognisable here, particularly the cinema, which has a huge terrace on its roof with a gate and fountain.

The dominant building on Bankowy Square is the Azure Tower (*Błękitny Wieżowiec*) on the corner of Solidarności Avenue. Nearby, is a monument to Stefan Stażyński, the mayor of Warsaw who was killed by the Nazis. He holds a map of the city, which is sometimes said to look like his coat.

Another monument depicts the arch-representative of Polish Romanticism Juliusz Słowacki, and this is certainly not a controversial addition to the square. Before Słowacki, the plinth was occupied by Feliks Dzierżyński, also known as 'Iron Felix', a Polish revolutionary in the service of Russian communists. He was the founder of the inauspicious Russian Extraordinary Commission to Combat Counter-revolution and Sabotage, or *Cheka*.

While the eastern side of the square is filled with humdrum architecture, the western and south frontages are absolutely splendid. One building with a colonnade is a department of the local authority, gold-and-red flags waving above the entrance. Corazzi also designed this building together with the building on the corner of Elektoralna Street, which was once the home of the Polish Bank and Stock Exchange. Today, the green-domed edifice is occupied by the John Paul II Museum Collection (*Muzeum Kolekcji im. Jana Pawła II*) also known as the Porczyński Gallery (*Galeria Porczyńskich*). The collection includes paintings from the 15th to 19th centuries. The Saski Hotel

adjoins the gallery to the south.

Opposite the Saski Hotel, on the corner of Senatorska Street, is the Azure Palace (*Błękitny Pałac*). This name, unfortunately, is deceiving! In the past, it was truly blue and rococo, later being remodelled in the classical style with harmonious proportions and elegance, today however it is a drab structure. Its occupants were the magnates of the Zamoyski and Czartoryski families, not to mention the beautiful Anna Orzelska, illegitimate daughter of King August II Wettin. The palace consists of several sections and through one of its buildings the Saski Garden (*Ogród Saski*) may be reached. In the wing on the Senatorska Street side there is a Chinese restaurant, while in the main body the Office of Municipal Transportation is located.

Monument to Wojciech Bogusławski

Walk: Along Miodowa Street

In the 18th century, thirteen residences stood on Miodowa Street. Despite only half of this number surviving to the present day, there is still a great deal to see here. The Krakow Bishops' Palace (*Pałac Biskupów Krakowskich*) is well worth seeing, decorated as it is with allegories relating to science and war, while Małachowski Palace (*Pałac Małachowskich*), with its rococo facade and courtyard, is worthy of a visit.

Allow about 25 minutes

1 Pałac Branickich (Branicki Castle)

Branicki Castle (No. 6) was one of the most magnificent residences of 18th-century Warsaw. The late-baroque horseshoe-shaped castle with its courtyard, stretches up to Podwale Street from where the gate and classical outbuildings are visible. It was built in the 1740s and later remodelled in the 19th century. Just after the Second World War, between 1947 and 1953, it was again rebuilt, this time in line with the images of it found in paintings by Canaletto (see Royal Castle p42-3). The facade of the main building is adorned with allegorical sculptures relating to science and art.

Miodowa Street - where palaces find new purpose

2 Pałac Morsztynów (The Morsztyns Palace)

The residence at No.10 is a palace which has changed hands many times and been remodelled frequently according to the tastes of the various new owners. Its post-war restorers decided to return it to its 18th-century form.

3 Kościół Przemienienia Pańskiego Ojców Kapucynów (The Capuchin Franciscan Friars' Church of the

Transfiguration)

The baroque Church of the Transfiguration is famous for having a mechanical nativity scene, which has been operating since 1949. The Capuchin order was brought to Poland by King John III Sobieski. The church commemorates Sobieski's victory in the Polish-Turkish battles of Chocim in 1681 and Vienna in 1683, and the king's heart is held inside in a silver urn; his successor as king, August II Wettin (*August II Mocny*), is also interred here and rests in a marble urn.

4 Pałac L. Paca (Ludwik Pac Palace)

The building at No.15 Miodowa Street is occupied by the Ministry of Health and Welfare. The original palace was built for prince Dominik Radziwiłł in the 17th century, but later bought by General Ludwik Pac and remodelled according to the plans of E Marconi. Marconi closed the yard of the palace by adding wings to the existing building, as well as adding the half-ellipse gate with two passages.

5 Kościół Wniebowzięcia NMP Ojców Bazylianów (The Assumption of the Blessed Virgin Mary and St. Basil the Great Order Church)

The building at No.16 is the sole Greek Catholic church in Warsaw. The building does not resemble a church and the only signs revealing its true use are

the cross on top and the equilateral triangle with an eye in a tympanum, which symbolises the Holy Trinity.

6. The Collegium Nobilium

In 1740, Piarist monk and scholar Stanisław Konarski founded an exclusive school for the sons of the nobility, the curriculum including extensive courses in foreign languages, history, law, mathematics, physics and geography. Active until 1832 it shaped numerous notable Polish citizens. The building is now the Aleksander Zelwerowicz Theatre Academy and the Collegium Nobilium Theatre School, which organises the International Theatre School Festival, open to the public.

Address: Miodowa 22/26

Warsaw has been healing its post-war wounds for a considerable time and the last phase of this process is the filling out of the urban structure with new and reconstructed buildings. Especially interesting is the contemporary four-storey glass Palace of Justice *(Pałac Sprawiedliwości)*, a so-called 'intelligent' building, which was built on Krasiński Square for $56 million. In the eastern facade there are three statues, which symbolise faith, love and virtue. The structure was awarded the Platinum Driller in 2000.

A place gradually being covered by buildings is the area of Trzech Krzyży Square *(Plac Trzech Krzyży)*, with the luxurious Sheraton Hotel in Prusa Street and the cylindrical office block of BJS International on Solidarności Avenue.

Another modern building has been built by the Vistula River on Dobra Street. A favourite with Varsovians, it houses the Warsaw University Library with its five million or so books and 60,000 magazine titles in 50,000m^2 of storage space. The building in fact comprises two structures joined by a glass-covered space to be used for commercial purposes and has been rented out to cafés, restaurants and boutiques. This 'connector' is filled with climbing plants and creepers, the greenery giving the impression that it is lower than it actually is. The library is also famous for its two gardens, the upper (2,000m^2) and the lower (15,000m^2). The upper garden is divided into gold, silver and carmine-pink parts all linked with bridges and there is also a fish pond and stream. The gardens are open to visitors.

Architects often refer to Warsaw's historical architecture. Jabłonowski Palace on Teatralny Square, designed by J Fontana and D Merlini, was the town hall in the years 1773-85. After the war it was dismantled and a new palace built in the 1990s, the new building receiving copies of the old facade and the new tower being modelled on the old. The palace presently accommodates a banking centre.

A prize-winning building stands on Piłsudskiego Square. This is *Metropolitan,* designed by Sir Norman Foster. This building won the world's most prestigious award in 2004 in Cannes, MIPIM in the business centre category, as well as the

Platinum Driller and many others. *Metropolitan* is a seven-storey building offering 55,000m² of floor space with a main facade consisting of black granite boards, or *razor blades*, attached perpendicular to the surface of the wall and windows. The visual effect is stunning – if you stand square to the wall the building seems constructed of glass, yet the view from either side is of a granite wall.

Nothing, however, compares to the Palace of Culture and Science. This giant stands at a height of 234.5m and neither the Marriot Hotel, *Intaco II* on Chałubińskiego Street, nor the Warsaw Financial Centre can match it. Even the needle of the Daewoo Eastern Europe building on the corner of Solidarności Avenue and Towarowa Street falls short; the body of the Daewoo tower is at first angular, but at the halfway point becomes an impressive slim cylinder cut obliquely at its end.

Warsaw is a place of intense and extensive change in the landscape, with the largest number of prestigious developments having been sited in the north-western part of the city, among them the Atrium Tower and the Atrium and Babka Plazas. At present the city centre is expanding outwards from Marszałkowska Street and on towards Jana Pawła II Avenue and Towarowa Street.

Left: the courtyard of the Warsaw University Library
Upper right: *Metropolitan* – the multi-award-winning business centre
Bottom right: the new Jabłonowski Palace on Teatralny Square

Churches

The most attractive of the Warsaw's traditional churches can be found in the Old Town, in the New Town and along the Royal Tract *(Trakt Królewski)*, while the more modern churches are built in newer quarters of the city. The majority of the older churches were razed during the Second World War and later reconstructed in detail, including around 100 churches, convents and chapels, of which 90 percent are Roman Catholic.

The entrance to the St John the Baptist Cathedral

Katedra św. Jana Chrzciela (St John the Baptist Cathedral)

The history of this cathedral reaches back to the 13th century when a wooden chapel was added to the castle of the Dukes of Mazovia. Later, at the turn of the 15th century a new Gothic parish church was built, announced by the collegiate in 1798. In 1798 the building's status was changed as the church was declared a cathedral and then later, in 1817, became an arch-cathedral. This church/cathedral witnessed the Polish-Teutonic conflict, the coronations of Stanislaus Leszczyński and Stanislaus Augustus Poniatowski and the ratification of the Constitution of 3rd May. The cathedral was heavily damaged during the bombing in 1939, but total destruction came in 1944 at the time of the Warsaw Uprising. Fire-throwers and grenades were used in the battle between the rebels and German army and German tanks were twice driven inside. You'll see that the caterpillar tracks of the tank-mine named Goliath have been affixed to the wall of the rebuilt cathedral on the Kanonia Street side. The church's new facade was designed by Jan Zachwatowicz in the Gothic style. The crypts are a place of eternal peace for King Stanislaus Augustus Poniatowski, the writer Henryk Sienkiewicz, the pianist and Prime Minister Jan Ignacy Paderewski and Presidents Gabriel Narutowicz and Ignacy Mościski.

An element of especial interest is Boryczko's Chapel *(Kaplica Boryczków)*, which is covered with star vaulting and renowned for its miraculous Holy Cross from the 16th century. A rare feature is the figure of the crucified Jesus, which has real human hair; it was a gift from the rich tradesman Jurga Boryczko. There is also an epitaph board with a portrait of the chapel's founder, who died in 1643.

The tomb of a Marshal of the Diet, Stanisław Małachowski, is a precious monument made of white marble and designed by Danish sculptor Berthel Thorvaldsen. There is also a copy of a painting by Domenico Ghirlandaio entitled the *The Bow of Three Magi* and a chapel from the 1980s commemorating Primate Cardinal Stefan Wyszyński, who is also known as the Primate of the Millennium.

The cathedral has also been employed as a venue for concerts during the International Organ Music Festival.

In the 1990s the remains of the last king of Poland, Stanislaus Augustus Poniatowski, were moved from Ukraine to this cathedral. There is a prophecy in Poland that kings with the name Stanislaus attract outsider influences, which has been true since King Boleslaus II the Bold *(Bolesław II Śmiały)* ordered the killing of St Stanislaus, the bishop of Krakow in 1079. When Stanislaus Leszczyński was elected king, Swedish soldiers were present during the ceremony; Stanislaus Augustus Poniatowski was elected following a demonstration of Russian military power; Stanislaus Augustus Poniatowski himself was moved to Ukraine in the 1930s and in 1939 the German and Russian armies attacked Poland. Some believe that Poniatowski's return brought about the alliance with NATO, which seems to be a beneficial one for Poland.
Address: Świętojańska 8

Katedra Polowa NMP Królowej Korony Polskiej (Field Cathedral Church of the Polish Army)

This is a baroque Piartist monks' church built in 1660-82 by T Buratini and founded by King Johan II Casimir Vasa *(Jan Kazimierz)*. The interior is decorated with seven altars, paintings of illustrious artists and, between 1758 and 1769 the magnificent facade was added. From 1835-36 the church was remodelled into a Russian Orthodox Church with gold-plated Byzantine domes. After Poland regained her independence in 1918, the Orthodox church was once again remodelled and from 1923-33 was returned to Catholicism and designated as a military church, its original appearance and furnishings restored. After the Second World War, in the years 1946-60, it was rebuilt in the baroque style and declared a field cathedral in 1991, the anchor as a symbol of the navy and the propeller, a symbol of the air force were placed in front of the building. Plaques commemorating soldiers who died on all fronts of the Second World War were unveiled, and in the vestibule are the names of members of the Polish Legions. There is also the statue *Jesus Christ of the Missing* by Mirosław Biskupski. Opposite the cathedral you'll find a monument to the Warsaw Uprising.
Address:. Długa 13/15

Inside the Field Cathedral of the Polish Army

Kościół św. Ducha i Klasztor Paulinów (The Church of the Holy Ghost and Pauline Monastery)

The baroque church standing at No.23 Nowomiejska has been a starting point for the annual pilgrimages to the spiritual capital of Poland, Częstochowa, since 1711. The present church was constructed between 1707-11 accordingly to replace the previous building, which burned down in 1655 and has since been rebuilt after the Second World War. It is a two-storey building with a plain facade and two high towers. The pilasters are ornamented with cornices and niches containing figures of the saints. The Pauline Monastery was founded in 1671 on the corner of Podwale Street and for several years was managed by Father Augustyn Kordecki, famed for his role in the successful defence of the convent in Częstochowa against the Swedish army.

Address: Nowomiejska 23

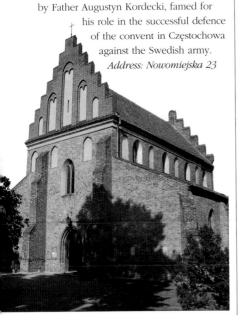

The Church of the Marian Visitation

Kościół św. Jacka i Klasztor Dominikanów (St Hyacinth's Church and the Dominican Convent)

The combined St Hyacinth's Church and Dominican Convent are regarded as the largest sacral complex in Warsaw and were probably built by Joannes Italus between 1612 and 1638. The original church possessed fourteen altars and five chapels. In 1944 it was adapted as a hospital, treating injured insurgents of the Uprising, who were killed by bombing when 90 percent of the church was demolished. However, it was rebuilt in the years 1947-59; the tympanum above the main entrance shows the Mother of God, St Dominic and St Hyacinth, while the unusual combination of the Gothic and early baroque styles in stucco works in the side naves are of particular interest.

The most valuable monument is the baroque tomb chapel of Adam and Małgorzata Kotowski, which was built in 1691-94. Adam Kotowski was a peasant who escaped to Warsaw, made a fortune and bought his way into the nobility. The chapel was designed by the notable Dutch architect Tylman van Gameren and was the sole original element to survive the Second World War. Its interior is home to a painting depicting the Holy Mother of God with the baby Jesus, as well as marble epitaphs with effigies of the founders painted on a sheet of metal. In the left-hand nave there is also a tablet commemorating Italian and British parachutists who died fighting for Polish independence.

Address: Freta 8/10

St Casimir's Church of the Benedictines of the Perpetual Adoration of the Blessed Sacrament

Kościółśw. Marcina (St Martin's Church)

Founded for the Augustinian Order in 1354 and destroyed during the Second World War, it was reconstructed in the baroque, although its furnishings are modern and designed by Sister Alma Skrzydlewska. A feature that survived the war is the cross, partially burned, which is now located in the central nave. This church was chosen as a meeting place for Polish nobleman in the 16th century and became the site of theological discussions and political disputes, which often ended in duels. In the 1980s it became a symbol of the Solidarity movement's resistance to the communist regime and was in the charge of the Franciscan Servants of the Cross, who managed an extraordinary school for blind children in the village of Laski near Warsaw. The church is worth visiting on 28th August when the very first Polish national anthem, entitled *Bogurodzica*, is sung in Old Polish and the interior is lit only by candles. The church is the eternal resting place of the court musician, composer, musician *Sacrae Regis Maestatis*, writer and poet Adam Jarzębski, who served King Ladislas IV Vasa *(Władysław IV Waza)*.
Address: Piwna 9/11

Kościół NMP Łaskawej i Klasztor Jezuitów (Holy Virgin Mary the Merciful Church and Jesuit Monastery)

This baroque church is not far from the St John the Baptist Cathedral and is easily recognisable owing to the baroque stone figure of a bear, carved in 1762-64 by J Plersch, standing in front of the entrance.

The interior of the Holy Cross Church

This one-naved church has the highest oval-domed tower in the Old Town and is devoted to the Holy Virgin Mary the Merciful, the patron saint of Warsaw. The church and monastery were built for the Jesuit monks between 1609 and 1626, and having been totally destroyed in the Second World War, were reconstructed down to the smallest detail. The main treasures are the painting of the *Holy Mary the Merciful*, which was presented to King Johan II Casimir Vasa *(Jan Kazimierz)* by the Pope in 1651, and the Gothic cross dating from the 16th century; in the crypt of the church there is a *lapidarium* protecting parts of the grave of the statesman Jan Tarło. The church was visited twice by Pope John Paul II, while a plaque near the entrance commemorates the Polish Primate of the Millennium, Cardinal Stefan Wyszyński, as well as the Pope himself.
Address: Świętojańska 10

KościółNawiedzenia NMP (Church of the Marian Visitation)

According to legend, the Mother of God appeared to a rich but childless miller, who asked her for a son. The Holy Mother asked him to build a church where he saw a snowcapped hill and to baptise the son he was to have in the newly built place of worship. The miller found a hill with a partially-built church and erected a bell tower there, and the very next year he became a father. The church was confirmed in 1411 by a duchess, Anna of Mazovia and marble sculptures were brought from Italy. A precious painting showing the scene of the Marian Visitation hangs in the left-hand chapel, painted by the 'Silesian Rembrandt' Michael Leopold Willmann in the 17th century. The church was damaged many times by the Swedes in the 17th century and demolished by the Germans in 1944. In 1981, in the period of martial law, the church was the scene of patriotic performances and there is also a monument to the patriot Walerian Łukasiński, the founder of the National Patriotic Society.
Address: Przyrynek 2

Kościółśw. Jana Bożego i Klasztor Bonifratrów (Church of the Hospitaller Brothers of St John of God)

This church was built in the years 1724-26 by the architects J Fontana and A Solari. In following St John of God, the monks sought the poor and the sick on the streets of Warsaw to be treated and taken care of in their hospital. The most illustrious physician was Brother Ludwik Perzyna who authored several books on surgery, obstetrics, anatomy and health education.

Highly-skilled monks were sent to wars, to all fronts of the national uprisings of 1831 and 1963 and to the Warsaw Uprising. Although the hospital was razed and never rebuilt, the church was reconstructed following damage. Between the 1980s and early 1990s, the monks managed a special consultancy offering herbal medicines. Not far from the church is the monument to the Dead and Murdered in the East (Pomnik Poległych i Pomordowanych na Wschodzie), unveiled in 1995.
Address: Bonifraterska 12

Kościół św. Aleksandra (St Alexander's Church)
See Aleje Ujazdowskie p88-93

Kościółśw. Anny i Klasztor Bernardynów (St Anna and Bernardine Church)
See Krakowskie Przedmieście and Nowy Świat Streets, p68

Kościół św. Benona (St Benno of Meissen Church); Kościół św. Franciszka Serafickiego (St Francis Seraph Church); Kościół św. Kazimierza i Klasztor Sakramentek (St Casimir's Church and the Convent of the Benedictines of the Perpetual Adoration of the Blessed Sacrament)

See Walk: Around the New Town Market Square, p48

Kościół św. Krzyża (Holy Cross Church); KościółNawiedzenia NMP (Church of the Marian Visitation)
See Walk: Around the University, p74-5

KościółMatki Boskiej Nieustającej Pomocy (Church of the Holy Mother of God of Everlasting Help); KościółMatki Boskiej Zwycięskiej (Church of the Holy Mother of God the Victorious)
See Saska Kępa, p142-143

The Assumption of the Holy Mother of God and St Joseph the Bridegroom Church

The classical facade of St Anna's church

Krakowskie Przedmieście and Nowy Świat Streets

The streets south of the Old Town, which carried travellers into Warsaw from Krakow, were collectively named the Royal Tract *(Trakt Królewski)*; the Tract now runs from the Royal Castle, along Krakowskie Przedmieście Street, Nowy Świat Street, the Ujazdowskie Avenues and Sobieskiego Street to arrive finally at Wilanów Palace. Palaces, churches, houses and governmental and university buildings have all been built on Krakowskie Przedmieście and Nowy Świat Streets at one time or another.

The first summer residences of rich Varsovians and the Polish kings were built along Krakowskie Przedmieście Street, among the beautiful gardens on the edge of the Varsovian Scarp by the Vistula. During the Polish-Swedish War in the 1650s dozens of palaces and townhouses were razed, today's architecture being predominantly the result of reconstruction performed after the Second World War. At that time Warsaw's architecture was rebuilt in the 17th- and 18th-century styles and the townhouses in Nowy Świat were returned to their classical forms. The ground floors of the townhouses are occupied by brand-name boutiques, galleries, cafés, perfumeries and restaurants with summer gardens.

Kościół św. Anny i klasztor Bernadrynów (St Anna's Church and the Convent of Bernhard)

The church was founded in the 15th century by Duchess Anna of Mazovia who brought the Bernhard monks to

Warsaw from Krakow. In 1505 the church was destroyed by fire, but rebuilt in 1511 as a far larger and more attractive building. The building was extended between 1513-14, when it received the cell-vaulting that can still be seen today. After the next fire, in 1515, duchess Anna Radziwiłłówna founded a new church; sadly this too was burned in turn in 1657 during the Polish-Swedish War and Hungarian invasion.

The church was remodelled and rebuilt many times, but was also famous for music. *Bon tone* and good manners of the second half of the 18th century required spending Sunday afternoons at *belle messe, belle musique* (beautiful Holy Mass, beautiful music), and at concerts organised to celebrate St Cecile.

The church also protects the grave of the patron of Warsaw *Władysław z Goleniowa* (Władysław from Goleniów). The Blessed Władysław was a famous orator and preacher, poet, Bernhard monk and author of popular passion songs, who, according to legend, became so excited when giving a sermon on Good Friday in

1505 that he fell into a trance and began to levitate, floating above the pulpit. The church was endangered by the construction of the East-West Route *(Trasa W-Z)* in 1949, the watery unstable ground under the church slipping and the walls cracking. It was saved by Professor Romuald Cebertowicz, the inventor of the so-called electro-osmosis method, also known as cebertisation, who helped to petrify the soil using chemical salts. Two electrodes were installed in the ground and by use of direct current the soil grew dry and solid, the electrodes working rather like pumps. In addition, the whole structure of the building was reinforced with special ferroconcrete constructions. Cebertowicz's electro-osmosis was also used to save the Leaning Tower of Pisa in Italy. Now the church is labelled 'Academic' and serves the city's students. It is famed as a superb venue for marriage ceremonies, young people believing that all couples married in St Anna's live a happy life together.

Address: Krakowskie Przedmieście 68

Pomnik Adama Mickiewicza (Monument to Adam Mickiewicz)

Adam Mickiewicz (1798-1855), the Romantic Polish national poet, was the author of the Polish national poem *Pan Tadeusz*, as well as lyrics, sonnets and ballads and the renowned *Forefathers' Eve (Dziady)*, among many other works. The statue was sculpted in 1898 by Cyprian Godebski, with the plinth the work of Józef Pius Dziekoński and Władysław Marconi. The construction of the monument required the permission of the Russians, and they agreed, though with one condition: the monument could not be larger than the statue of Iwan Paskiewicz, the Russian field marshal who crushed the November Uprising in 1931; Mickiewicz's bronze figure was indeed smaller, yet the plinth was built higher. The monument was unveiled in 1898 to the sounds of the *Prayer (Modlitwa)* by Stanisław Moniuszko, the Polish national composer, while the speech was given by the Polish national novelist, the Nobel prize-winning Henryk Sienkiewicz. The ceremony concluded with a peaceful demonstration. A feature of the monument also worthy of attention is the hand-forged and beaten fence, a gift from Varsovian workers. In 1968 the area near the monument was the scene of student protests against the order to remove posters for the performance of Mickiewicz's *Forefathers Eve (Dziady)* directed by Kazimierz Dejmek (also see p23 and 53).

Figura Matki Boskiej Passawskiej (Statue of the Holy Mother of God the Passau)

This baroque statue, standing close to the monument to Adam Mickiewicz, commemorates an incredible coincidence: the victory of John III

The monument to Adam Mickiewicz

Sobieski at the Siege of Vienna in 1683 and the the royal family's miraculous salvation from plague. Created by the Italian artist S Bellotti, the statue shows the Holy Mother holding the baby Jesus and a sceptre, and relates to the Marian cult of the Passau region of Bavaria in Germany and the miraculous statue of the Holy Mother of Altötting which provided protection from plague. Warsaw's figure happily survived the war, the sole landmark to do so in this area.

The Dziekanka Dormitory

This is a dark pink building with a huge opening in the main facade giving access to horse-drawn vehicles, built in 1770-84 on land belonging to the dean (*Dziekan*) of the St John Cathedral collegiate. Around 1830 this manor was remodelled into an inn, and after rebuilding following the Second World War it became a dormitory and centre of student cultural life. It is known for artistic performances, art exhibitions, musical events and

Dziekanka in Krakowskie Przedmieście Street

festivals such as the Garden Theatre Festival. *Address: Krakowskie Przedmieście 56*

Pomnik księcia Józefa Poniatowskiego (Prince Józef Poniatowski Monument)

This monument, sculpted by the Danish artist Berthel Thorvaldsen, stands before the Governor's Palace (*Pałac Namiestnikowski, see Palaces p76-81*). Prince Józef Poniatowski was a hero of the Napoleonic Wars who died in 1813 at the Battle of Leipzig by drowning in the Elster river. In 1813 a special organisational committee decided to found a monument to him, and this was at first placed at Modlin fortress, about 35km from Warsaw, but in 1840 was moved to the home of Field Marshal Paskiewicz in Gomel in Belarus. The monument of the mounted prince, wearing a Roman tunic, was brought back to Poland in 1922 only to be destroyed during the Second World War. After extensive repair in Denmark it was presented as a gift to Varsovians by the citizens of Copenhagen, taking up its present position.
Address: Krakowskie Przedmieście 46/48

Hotel Bristol

The luxurious Bristol Hotel was built in 1899-1901 in the neo-Renaissance style. It has played host to many celebrities and has witnessed everything from the celebration of Maria Skłodowska-Curie's receiving the Nobel prize and Marshal Piłsudski's receptions to the world-famous opera singer Jan Kiepura who sang his well-known line 'brunettes, blonds, all you girls I want to kiss.' In the 1930s the

The main gate of Warsaw University

painter Wojciech Kossak, famous for historical and battle scenes, had his studio at the hotel, using his paintings to pay the bill. Just after the 1993 opening, the hotel hosted the former British Prime Minister Margaret Thatcher, and Queen Elizabeth II held a dinner party. Other notable guests include the French President Jacques Chirac and the famous Spanish opera singer José Carreras.
Address: Krakowskie Przedmieście 46/48

Uniwersytet Warszawski (Warsaw University)

In 1634 King Johan Casimir Vasa *(Jan Kazimierz)* built a palace named the Villa Regia, also known as Kazimierzowski Palace *(Pałac Kazimierzowski)*, which became his favourite residence. After rebuilding it was adopted as a school and when the foundation of the University was announced in 1816 the building became its seat. The tsar had accepted the institution with its five departments, law and administration, medicine, philosophy, theology and fine art, but

after the November Uprising the University was closed as the majority of students had participated in the rebellion. In 1859 the tsar agreed to open a School of Medicine and Surgery, and to this another three departments were added, allowing the University to begin admitting students again. During the Second World War the German occupiers forbade teaching, yet the professors continued to hold lectures in private buildings, creating an underground education system involving about 300 professors and 3,500

The famous and luxurious Bristol Hotel

students, from which body 63 professors were to die. Following the war, in December 1945, about four million students began studying. At present Kazimierzowski Palace contains the Rector's Office; the main entrance to the building is ornate, with two statues standing in niches, on the right Victoria, on the left Urania, while above the main gate there is a crowned eagle surrounded by stars, holding in its claws sprigs of olive and laurel. The University admits students to 18 departments, with 25 interdisciplinary centres organising courses.

Address: Krakowskie Przedmieście 26/28

Hotel Europejski

On 30th June, 2005 this famous hotel was closed, but its beginnings can be traced back to the years 1855-77, when it was built piece by piece to become the first modern hotel in Warsaw, a meeting place

The facade of the Europejski Hotel

for the cream of Varsovian society, as well as artists and politicians. This heyday lasted until 1944, when it was ruined but the reconstruction re-established the neo-Renaissance facade and interior. It has been taken over from the Orbis hotel chain by the ancestor of its pre-war owner, the duchess Maria Anna Czetwertyńska, the new owner looking for an investor such as Ritz-Carlton or Regent International Hotels. According to the plans made public, it may become a five-star hotel.

Address: Krakowskie Przedmieście 13

Pomnik Mikołaja Kopernika (Nicholas Copernicus Monument)

This landmark is located at Staszic Palace. The raising of funds for its construction began in 1810, however it was not until 1830 that it was sculpted by the remarkable Danish artist Berthel Thorvaldsen. Nicholas Copernicus was born in Toruń in Poland in 1473 and is famed for his heliocentric theory, and here the astronomer is shown with an *astrolabium* in his left hand and a compass in his right. During war the Germans covered the monument's Polish inscriptions with German tablets, yet these were removed in a sabotage action by a scout named Alek Dawidowski, and when the monument was moved to western Poland for scrapping, it was miraculously saved and returned to Warsaw. Two other monuments were cast from the same mould, one located in Montreal in Canada, the second in Chicago in the USA.

Address: Krakowskie Przedmieście

The A Blikle café on Nowy Świat Street

Cukiernia A.Bliklego (The A Blikle Café)

Five generations of Antoni Kazimierz Blikle's family have been in the confectionery business since their cake shop was founded in 1869, on Nowy Świat Street. A meeting place for artists, actresses worked as waitresses during the war, and it was and still is famous for the best Varsovian *pączki*–glazed doughnuts with rose jam filling. In 1993, Andrzej Blikle opened this café close to the original shop.
Address: Nowy Świat 33

Chmielna Street

During the interwar period (1918-1939) Chmielna Street was the place of renowned shops, cafés and summer courtyard theatres, and after the war it became synonymous with Varsovian folklore, propagated by the Orchestra from Chmielna *(Orkiestra z Chmielnej)*. The name of the street was changed to Rutkowskiego and it became a place of commissions, of private shops selling solid shoes, clothing, wedding dresses and handicraft products. Now the street is a pedestrianised promenade full of small boutiques and well-known stores, where in summer the owners of the cafés put tables outside and socialising blooms.

Dom Partii (House of the Polish United Workers' Party (PZPR))

At the junction of Nowy Świat Street and Jerozolimskie Avenue, near the de Gaulle roundabout, there is a quadrilateral complex of white buildings which once belonged to the Polish United Workers' Party (PZPR). Designed in 1948, this is a typical example of 'monumentalism'. In the 1990s the building became the largest eastern-European stock exchange and it is now a modern banking and finance centre hosting several prestigious companies.
Address: Nowy Świat 6

Walk: Around the University

The neighbourhood of Warsaw University shelters a number of palaces, churches and townhouses, making it an attractive destination for tourists. In addition, the thousands of students attending this leading Polish university create an atmosphere pulsating with life, which only the summer holidays can subdue. *Allow 40 minutes.*

1 Kościół Opieki św. Józefa i klasztor Wizytek (Church of St Joseph's Care and Convent of the Sisters of the Marian Visitation)

The construction of the first wooden church on this site was begun around 1654 by Queen Marie Louise Gonzaga de Nevers; the second brick church rose gradually over the period 1728-65, the slow pace caused by issues arising from a miscalculation of the weight of its domes. Happily, the church went on to survive the Second World War and has remained unchanged in its late-baroque and rococo style. Particularly eye-catching features are the white interior, the boat-shaped pulpit and the angel holding a sail; the pulpit

Atlantes supports a balcony -Tyszkiewicz Palace

symbolises the institution of the Church, sailing on through storms that beset it.
Address: Krakowskie Przedmieście 34

2 Pałac Tyszkiewiczów (Tyszkiewicz Palace)

This palace was built for Ludwik Tyszkiewicz in 1792 and is regarded as one of the most delightful classical buildings in Warsaw, crowned by a cartouche presenting the Potocki family coat of arms, they having bought the palace from the Tyszkiewicz family in 1840. The palace now hosts the Old Print and Drawing Office.
Address: Krakowskie Przedmieście 32

3 Pałac Czapskich (Czapski Palace)

This palace was constructed in 1713-18 to become home to a number of notable families. In 1826 Fryderyk Chopin's parents rented a flat there and visitors today may admire his parlour. At present the palace is the seat of the Academy of Fine Arts and its courtyard is decorated with a copy of the famous monument to *Condolieri, Capitano Generale della Repubblica Veneta Bartolomeo Calleoni,* who was the commander of an army of mercenaries

fighting for Venice. Sculpted by Florentine artist Andrea del Verrocchio (his original standing in Venice) this copy was cast in Szczecin in Poland for the local National Museum's collection of Renaissance monuments, but transferred to Warsaw to complement the collection of medieval art.
Address: Krakowskie Przedmieście 5

4 Pałac Uruskich (Uruski Palace)

Uruski Palace was constructed in 1744-47 for S Uruski, a count who bought his aristocratic title. This present building is not the first however, as there was once a palace here belonging to the father of Stanislaus Augustus Poniatowski, the last king of Poland. It was in that building that Stanislaus learnt of his election as king, an event commemorated by a monument standing in the courtyard.
Address: Krakowskie Przedmieście 30

5 Kościół św. Kryża (Holy Cross Church)

This is an easily-recognisable building owing to a black monument of Christ bearing a cross with the inscription *Sursum Corda* ('Lift up your hearts'). Built in the years 1679-96, its most precious treasure is the urn

containing the heart of the Polish national composer Fryderyk Chopin, which is embedded in the first pillar on the left in the main nave. The heart was brought from France to Warsaw by Chopin's sister Ludwika, the young Frederyk having come to play the organ here. Another urn holds the heart of the Nobel prize-winning writer Władysław Reymont. The church was, and still is, famous for patriotic performances, and as a result the epitaphs of several notable Poles may be found here, for instance those of the writer B Prus, the poets J I Kraszewski and J Słowacki, and General W Sikorski.
Address: Krakowskie Przedmieście 3

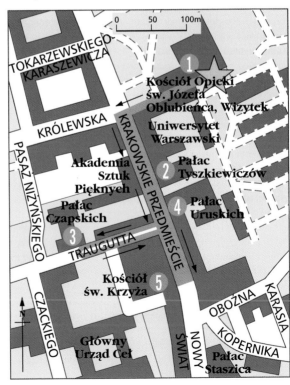

Palaces

In the 17th and 18th centuries kings and magnates alike built palaces in Warsaw in the most attractive of locations, the Old and New Towns. In architectural terms, three main types of palace may be observed: the free standing, the U-shaped with their open yards and those standing alongside a street.

Pebendowski-Radziwiłèłè Palace

The free standing palaces and the U-shaped were modelled on the French complexes comprising a palace and a park, and in front of the main body is a courtyard surrounded by a high ornamented fence. The majority of these palaces were built in the 17th century and extended later. In the first half of the 17th century Radziwiłłand the Primate's Palace were of the freestanding type, although they were later turned into three-winged palaces with courtyards opening onto the side facing the street.

Palaces erected alongside a street have inner courtyards and gardens at the rear. The sole difference between the magnates' and the burghers' palaces were their size, those of the magnates being larger and having more decorative facades. Palaces of this type are Kossakowski, Tyszkiewicz, Uruski and A Zamoyski; S Staszic's 19th-century palace on Krakowskie Przedmieście Street has a completely different appearance. Now the palaces give themselves up for use by the University, by national institutions and scientific institutes, and by museums and galleries.

Gnińskich-Ostrogskich Palace and the F Chopin Society

Built in 1681-85 as a part of a larger residence, it was here in the cellars that, according to legend, the Gold Duck lived (see *Varsovian Legends* p24-5). In 1859 the palace became the home of the Warsaw Academy of Music, after which it was turned into the seat of the F Chopin Society, best known for organising the F Chopin International Piano Contest, initiated in 1927 by Professor Żurawlew. Regular concerts are performed in the concert hall and there is also the F Chopin Museum with items belonging to the composer. Chopin was born in Żelazowa Wola near Warsaw and as a young boy was educated in Warsaw. He left Poland forever in 1830 to travel to Paris. The exhibition contains Chopin's letters, portraits, autographs and the piano which was used for the two last years of his life. Here also is the studio of Professor Żurawlew, pianist and judge of the International Piano Contest.
Address: Okólnik 1

Kossakowski Palace

Built in the late 18th century by E Schroeger for the banker I Ollier, and rebuilt in the Italian Renaissance style in 1849-51 by E Marconi, the time of this palace's greatest architectural splendour came with Count S Kossakowski's residence. He organised his famous Literary Fridays, which were meetings of the intellectual elite, and visitors to the palace could study one of the best collections of paintings in Poland. In 1882 the Polish impressionist painter Władysław Podkowiński had his studio here, and in that time created several unique views of Nowy Świat Street. The palace was rebuilt for the last time between 1949 and 1950 in the neo-classical style.

Address: Nowy Świat 19

Pałac Namiestnikowski/Pałac Prezydencki (Governor's or Presidential Palace)

This palace was built in the 17th century for Commander S Koniecpolski and later adapted to be the seat of the Russian tsar's governor, General Józef Zajączek. No less well-known in Warsaw than the general was his wife, a famous ballerina, who scandalised Varsovian society with her numerous romances. Another story concerns the four lions guarding the main gate: they are said to roar only when a truly chaste woman passes by.

Later, the building was designated as

The Governor's Palace, the residence of the President of Poland

the seat of the Council of Ministers and
since 1994 it has been a residence for
Polish presidents. The palace has
witnessed several historical moments. In
1955 the Warsaw Pact was signed here,
and in 1974 the treaty regulating Polish-
German relations, while in 1989 the
palace hosted the Round Table debates
between the representatives of the
communist regime and its political
opponents. The first political party was
also formed here, the Congress of the
Constitution of 3rd May, gathering in
1791-92. In front of the palace is a
monument to Duke Józef Poniatowski.
Address: Krakowskie Przedmieście 46/48

Zamoyski Palace on Foksal Street

Pałac Potockich (Potocki Palace)

This two-storey square palace was built
in the 1760s for Duke Aleksander
Czartoryski and, after its remodelling by
the famous architects S B Zug and J C
Kamsetzer, was bought by the Potocki
family in 1799, the reason for the presence
of the Potocki coat of arms on the
tympanum. The palace was the venue of
the famous ball in honour of Napoleon
Bonaparte on 22nd January 1807. The
French Caesar danced with his Polish
muse, the 21-year-old Countess Maria
Walewska, who became his official
maitresse and bore him a son. It was the
beautiful Maria who was chosen by Polish
patriots as the intermediary between them
and Napoleon, the root of great problems.
In the 19th century exhibitions of Polish
painting were held in the palace, with
works showing scenes from Polish history,
such as *Prussian Homage* (*Hołd Pruski*)
or *The Battle of Grunwald* (*Pod
Grunwaldem*) by the marvellous Jan
Matejko, seen for the first time by

Varsovians. Having undergone post-war
remodelling, the building became the seat
of Ministry of Culture and Art.
Address: Krakowskie Przedmieście 15

Pałac Prymasowski (Primate's Palace)

This old 16th-century manor was converted
into a palace in 1691 for Primate Michał
Radziejowski and for 200 years thereafter it
was home to Polish Primates, the highest
officials of the Catholic Church. The palace
changed in appearance between 1777 and
1783 when it received magnificent stucco
works and was extended by the addition of
new galleries and pavilions. The palace
burned down in 1939 but was restored in
the years 1949-53 to its classical 18th-
century state. The most impressive feature
is the Great Hall (*Sala Wielka*) with its
gorgeous stucco works and Ionian
columns. The building was designated as
the seat of Ministry of Culture and Art,
although now it is the property of a
national company operating in
entertainment industry.
Address: Senatorska 13/15

Pałac Przebendowskich-Radziwiłłów (Przebendowski-Radziwiłł Palace)

This late-baroque three-storey palace is easily recognisable for its oval shape of the frontal part. It was built in 1728 for the crown treasurer, while another owner was the Spanish deputy Pedro Aranda, the founder of the Spanish Lodge of Freemasons.

In the early 20th century the palace was bought by the Radziwiłł family, who stayed until 1944, then after World War II it was rebuilt to house the Lenin Museum, though only for a short time. In 1990 it became the Museum of Independence, documenting Polish history from the three partitions to the present day.

Address: Aleja Solidarności 62

Pałac S. Staszica (S Staszic's Palace) / Polska Akademia Nauk (Polish Academy of Science)

This palace was erected in the years 1820-23 in the late-neo-classical style by the illustrious Italian architect Antonio Corazzi, the designer of the Great Theatre, the co-founder being S Staszic, scholar, philosopher and writer. The building was home to the Royal Scientific Society but after the November Uprising it was confiscated, and between 1892-93 was remodelled in Russian-Byzantine style to become a school. When Poland regained her independence in 1918 the palace's original classical appearance was restored and after rebuilding following the Second World War it now hosts the Polish Academy of Science and Warsaw

The facade of the Primate's Palace on Senatorska Street

Scientific Society.
Address: Nowy Świat 72

Pałac Andrzeja Zamoyskiego (A Zamoyski Palace)

Enrico Marconi established this neo-Renaissance palace in years 1843-46. The building was to witness a renowned incident recorded by the Romantic poet Cyprian Kamil Norwid in his work *Chopin's Piano (Fortepian Chopina)*. The incident being the attempted assassination of the tsar's governor F F Berg in 1864, followed by Russian soldiers taking revenge by plundering the palace and throwing the piano out of a window. This was no ordinary piano but one previously owned by Frederyk Chopin, and Norwid accurately pointed out that the 'ideal reached the pavement'. After World War II the palace became home to the University's Journalism Department.
Address: Nowy Świat 67/69

Pałac Zamoyskich (Zamoyski Palace)

Konstanty Zamoyski founded this palace in 1875-77 on Foksal Street. It was designed by L Marconi in a rare 17th-century style,

The Ballroom of the Palace on the Water

Potocki Palace on Krakowskie Przedmieście

typical of the French Renaissance era of Henry IV and Louis XIII. The palace is located in a picturesque park and was famous for balls and diplomatic receptions. It was here in 1923 that the Zamoyski family entertained the French Marshal Ferdinand Foch, who was honoured with the title of Marshal of Poland and with the nation's highest military decoration, *Virtuti Militari,* which can be compared to the British Victoria Cross or American Medal of Honour. The palace was reconstructed in 1946 after being completely devastated by war, and since 1965 one of its pavilions has provided space for the contemporary art of the Foksal Gallery *(Galeria Foksal). Address: Foksal 1/2/4*

Czapski, Tyszkiewicz and Uruski Palaces

(see Walk: Around the University p74-5)

The Palace on the Water

(see Walk: The Łazienkowski Garden p96)

Kazimierzowski Palace

(see Krakowskie Przedmieście and Nowy Świat Streets p68-73)

Raczyński and Sapieha Palaces

(see The New Town p44-7)

The Palaces at Natolin and Wilanów, and Królikarnia, Rozkosz and F Szuster's Palaces

(see Getting Away p138-143)

The building at the end of Kozia Street

Streets and Squares

In cities which have developed harmoniously the city centre always lies near the historical centre, yet Warsaw moved quickly from the role of a provincial town to that of the capital city. This city has simply outgrown its historical centre, as a child outgrows a school uniform and, it could not be decided which area of the city should be the new heart.

When King Sigismund III Vasa transferred the capital from Krakow to Warsaw the centre was clearly Zamkowy Square, an area usually only visited by Varsovians and tourists when participating in cultural events or on a Sunday stroll.

During the reigns of the Wettin dynasty the centre moved to Krakowskie Przedmieście and Miodowa Streets, where the residences of the magnates were built. This means that Kozia Street, the narrow link between Krakowskie Przedmieście and Miodowa, is well worth a visit to see the gardens of the Primate's Palace on one side and on the other a full row of these great houses. Of the two streets, Krakowskie Przedmieście is still a busy, lively destination.

The vigorously expanding town had no remarkable squares, the first appearing only in the 18th century when the Krasiński's courtyard was turned into Krasiński Square and made accessible to the public. In the 19th century the fences of Saski Palace were removed and this courtyard became a square too. Both were incorporated into the larger urban system

when Warsaw began developing in the west.

From Krakowskie Przedmieście the steep Bednarska Street descends, beginning near the Caritas Office which provides humanitarian aid both in Poland and abroad. The street has borne its present name since 1770, before which it was called Dung Street as all the waste of the city was transported along it en route to Dung Hill. Today Bednarska leads to the Mariensztad quarter around Mariensztad Street where the blocks of flats look older than they actually are (these buildings are not related to those of the oldest part of Warsaw). Similarly, the layout of the streets is not related to the system of the oldest part, having been brought into use on 22nd July 1949 as the first new quarter of the post-war city. Getting 'a little flat in Mariensztad' was the subject of the songs and dreams of young Varsovians. Mariensztad's market square became a place of festivals and entertainment, replacing the ruined city centre. The quarter's name comes from the historical character Maria Potocka, whose husband was the owner of the land and wished to honour his spouse by naming it after her. Unfortunately, this area beside the Vistula was a place of the local poor for many years.

Nowy Świat was always a quarter of entertainments and was enjoyed by the older among Warsaw's inhabitants and the post-war generation alike. Now it is an elegant promenade with limited traffic and many cafés and galleries. Nowy Świat is met by Foksal Street, the name of which commemorates London's Vauxhall Pleasure Gardens. Entertainment was provided here by the banker Franciszek Cabrit, who bought the gardens near Nowy Świat in 1776 for public events. The gardens were later divided into small lots, sold and the area densely built up.

Foksal Street is home to the neo-Renaissance palace of Konstanty Zamoyski, now hosting the Polish Architects' and Polish Artists' Societies and, in the pavilion that has been added to the palace, the Foksal Gallery (*Galeria Foksal*). Zamoyski Palace adjoins the Ministry of Foreign Affairs which is housed in a classical palace that once belonged to the Przeździecki family.

On the opposite side of Nowy Świat is Chmielna Street (see *Krakowskie Przedmieście and Nowy Świat Streets* p68-73), which in the years before the Second World War had the reputation of being occupied by prostitutes. After the war, when all trade was monopolised by the communist regime, private shops concentrated here, their shop windows displaying fashionable shoes and clothing, the desire of the woman of Warsaw. Chmielna Street retains its pre-war atmosphere in the music played by its street orchestras, regarded as the best in the city, who play the hits of that era as well as those from the period of the German occupation, the so-called 'forbidden songs'. Chmielna's image is now that of a fashionable, high-class street and a clean promenade of galleries and eating establishments in the yards at the rear.

On 14th January 1914 Warsaw received the new Poniatowski Bridge (*Most Poniatowskiego*) which elongated

Houses sit along the cobbles of Bednarska Street

Jerozolimskie Avenue across the Vistula, the city's centre of gravity moved once more. Jerozolimskie Avenue had already become a major artery of the urban plan in the 19th century, while before this it had been the route to the Jewish quarter, called New Jerusalem, which was located outside the limits of the city in what is now the area of Zawisza Square *(Plac Zawiszy)*.

The junction of Nowy Świat and Jerozolimskie Avenue was the location of the popular *Udziałowa* café, a meeting place for artists who came to read newspapers, gossip and debate. This tradition is maintained by EMPIK, one of a chain of stores with a great choice of Polish and foreign magazines, books and music, and good coffee to drink after a shopping expedition. On the opposite corner is the former seat of the PZPR Central Committee, the decision-making centre of the whole country under the previous political system, the PZPR being the Polish United Workers' Party. Ironically, the building has now become the Stock Exchange (Giełda Papierów Wartościowych).

Another major route is Marszałkowska Street, which regained its importance in the 19th century when it was extended as far as Bankowy Square. At one time Bankowy Square stood a chance of becoming Warsaw's elusive centre, yet this

The market square and houses in the Mariensztad quarter

honour eventually fell to the junction of Marszałkowska Street and Jerozolimskie Avenue with the construction of the Warsaw-Vienna railway station there in 1844-45. After the war the city's main railway station was moved a little further westwards, the old international terminus replaced by the *Centrum* underground station. For modern Warsaw, Marszałkowska Street is a place of commerce and communication. Its stone signpost showing the distances to European capitals was placed before the war.

The facades of Jerozolimskie Avenue are typical of the Secession (a form of Art Nouveau) style. One of the most attractive buildings is the *Polonia* hotel, which dates from early 20th century and after the Great War housed the French military mission led by General Charles de Gaulle. At the de Gaulle roundabout is the Forum hotel, which was the first Polish hotel to be incorporated into an international chain.

Looking south, the MDM quarter *(Marszałkowska Dzielnica Mieszkaniowa)* may be seen, built between 1952 and 1955 as a mixture of eclecticism and social realism. The MDM replaced demolished houses between Wilcza Street and Zbawiciela Square, and at its heart is Konstytucji Square. The social realist sculptures of a metallurgist, a miner and a female worker all wear the same face, but their different attributes reveal their professions.

Describing the centre of Warsaw requires mention of the vast Palace of Culture and Science, a landmark visible from every corner of the capital. Ask a Varsovian where the most beautiful view of the city may be found and the answer

Nowy Świat – street of shops and cafés

will be 'from the highest terrace of the Palace of Culture and Science' since only there is this architectural nightmare out of sight. The palace was designed by the Soviet architect Rudniew at the time of the worst communist terror, in the years 1952-55 and was modelled on Moscow's own social realist palaces. With a capacity of 817m³ and 3288 rooms, it hosts theatres and museums, offices and conference rooms, and international meetings, congresses and trade fairs as well as various institutions. There are also several good restaurants. The square on the Świetokrzyska Street side is given over in summer to basketball courts open to the public and free of charge, while in winter it is transformed into a skating rink. The view from the highest terrace is doubly attractive in that it takes in the fresh, adventurous and ever better architecture of contemporary Warsaw.

Warsaw was at the centre of the development of classicism in Poland, which took place during the reign of King Stanislaus Augustus Poniatowski. The style could be seen for the first time when the king was setting about remodelling the Royal Castle and Łazienki Park. Stanislaus Augustus Poniatowski was an educated king who held the ambition of creating an academy of fine art in Warsaw, together with a national museum. He invited a number of illustrious Italian architects and artists, and even the French architect Victor Louis, whose influence is visible in the designs of J Fontana and D Merlini.

One of the earliest examples of the classical style in Poland is the stone facade of the Church of the Assumption of the Holy Mother of God. This church was built in 1782, but had been designed 20 years earlier by Efraim Schroeger. It has a two-storey body with well-marked horizontal division and the centre is decorated with columns, the lower in the Toscanian order and the upper in the Corinthian. Between the columns there are two figures of Carmelite saints with medallions above, while a huge window divides the columns and illuminates the interior.

In 1777-83 E Schroeger himself rebuilt and extended the Primate's Palace (see *Palaces* p76-81), decorating the main body with a portico and adding rounded wings with pavilions and a portico on the courtyard side.

Also, a classical facade was designed for St Anna's Church, the work of C P Aigner and Stanisław Potocki (see *Churches* p62-7), to which in the 1820s the free-standing bell tower was added. Aigner was also creator of St Alexander's Church *(Kościół św. Aleksandra)*, which was built in 1818-25 on Trzech Krzyży Square and modelled on the Roman Pantheon. Also modelled on the Roman Pantheon, yet this time in 1777-81 by S B Zug, is a most remarkable church, the Evangelical-Augsburg church of the Holy Trinity *(Kościół Trójcy Świętej)* on Małachowskiego Square which is covered with a huge dome. C P Aigner was involved too with the huge Governor's Palace at No. 46-48 Krakowskie Przedmieście, which was rebuilt in the classical style in line with his plans in 1818-19.

In 1781-84 Merlini built the Assumption of the Blessed Virgin Mary and St Basil the Great Order Church at

No.16 Miodowa Street (see *Churches* p62-7), its octagonal body embedded between the walls of the monastery. The apse at the rear is effective, the facade is decorated with four Ionian pilasters and the whole is crowned with a cross in tympanum. In 1782-86 Merlini also produced a small domed palace called Królikarnia at No.113a Puławska. This was modelled on the famous *Villa Rotonda* near Vicenza in Italy, the best work of Andrea Palladio.

Kazimierzowski Palace at No.26-28 Krakowskie Przedmieście received the forms of late classicism in 1816 during the remodelling carried out on the seat of Warsaw University, and classical features are present in the outbuildings by J Kubicki dated 1814-16. A classical character is also attributed to the new Tyszkiewicz Palace, which was built in 1785-92 on Krakowskie Przedmieście Street.

In 1815, when the Polish Kingdom existed, economic growth allowed Warsaw to be more extensively shaped in the classical style. Several palaces and houses were erected on Krakowskie Przedmieście and Nowy Świat Streets, and in the years 1825-32 the Great Theatre was built by a graduate from the Florentine Academy of Fine Art, Antonio Corazzi. This building is regarded as one of the most beautiful classical buildings in Europe.

Left: sculpture on the facade of St Anna's Church
Right: the early-classical Myśliwiecki Palace in Łazienki park

Aleje Ujazdowskie

Ujazdowskie Avenues runs from Trzech Krzyży Square as far as Belwederska Street, elongating the Royal Tract southwards. The avenue was laid out between 1768 and 1773 during the reign of Stanislaus Augustus Poniatowski, although before this time there existed 'Passion Road' with stations commemorating the death of Christ. These had been founded by King August II Wettin in 1724-31 and were designed by J D Jauch in the Ujazdów quarter.

A Cracovian on a house in Mokotowska Street

Ujazdowskie Avenues *(Aleje Ujazdowskie)*, with its adjacent parks and gardens, is one of the most beautiful streets of Warsaw.

The classical St Alexander's Church on Trzech Krzyży Square

Among the palaces and patricians' houses, the Office of the Council of Ministers and Ujazdów Castle were both built on the scarp, while the area also contains the buildings of the Diet *(Sejm)* and governmental departments, as well as Belweder Palace with the monument to Marshal Józef Piłsudski.

Plac Trzech Krzyży (Three Cross Square)

According to pre-war guidebooks there were two columns topped with crosses built here in 1731, both having survived until today, as well as a third cross held by the Czech saint John of Nepomuk, who is present in a monument founded by Marshal Bieliński in 1752. The square was also formerly known as the Three Cross Crossroads or St Alexander's Square.

House No.2, the building abutting the modern shopping centre Holland Park, is home to the Institute for the Deaf-Mute and Blind founded by the priest and humanitarian Jakub Falkowski. There is also a monument to Prime Minister Wincenty Witos, the first to have come from the peasants' party.

Kościół św. Aleksandra (St Alexander's Church)

Built in 1818-25 and designed by C P Aigner, this church was constructed in place of a planned triumphal arch which was to have commemorated the arrival of the Russian tsar Alexander I who was crowned king and gave the Polish Kingdom a constitution.

The church's rotund classical body with its six-column portico makes reference to the Roman Pantheon. It was remodelled after World War II but in slightly changed form, the dome being a little lower. In the side altar is a baroque sculpture of Christ in the grave dating from the early 18th century. Priests from St Alexander's organise special services for the deaf-mute, while some masses are said in Latin.

Mokotowska Street

Mokotowska Street begins at Three Cross Square and runs towards Polna Street. It is an old route leading to the village of Raków, a village eventually incorporated into the larger urban structure. Today Mokotowska belongs with the well-preserved streets of old Warsaw. House No. 57 was built in 1900 with decoration depicting the Cracovian and the highlander. The house at No. 51-53 resembles a small palace with a courtyard and is a creation from the 1920s. House No.48, dated 1860, belonged to the writer Ignacy Kraszewski.

The modern Sheraton hotel

The facade of the Belweder, ceremonial palace for Polish Presidents

Gmachy Sejmu i Senatu (Diet and the Senate)

The traditions of Polish parliamentarism stretch back to the 15th century, however, the Polish parliament has not had but one home in history. It used to debate outside of Warsaw in the town of Piotrków, although when the Royal Castle was ready when the parliament returned to Warsaw. In 1918 the 19th-century building of the Maiden Education Institute was adapted to serve as the new seat of the parliament, and extended again in the years 1925-28 to house the Diet and Senate right up until 1939. In this last development the characteristic rounded hall used for the Diet's debates was created and decorated with reliefs in the art deco style. On 10th February 1919 the first convention of the Parliament of free Poland was held there, with two constitutions passed. In May 1926 Marshal Józef Piłsudski was chosen as Poland's president but he refused to accept the office.

Post-war reconstruction took place in the years 1949-52, overseen by B Pniewski, who developed the building further. In 1989 the Senate was re-established as the upper house of the parliament, having been dismissed by the communists. The building is open to visitors, who are able to view the Convocation Hall with the Presidential Box *(Sala Posiedzeń Sejmu i Loża Prezydenta)*, the Constitution of 3rd May and Maciej Rataj Presentation Halls *(Sale Rezprezentacyjne)*.

Address: Wiejska Street 2/4/6

The Houses of Ujazdowskie

Ujazdowskie Avenue is one of the most elegant streets in Warsaw with well-preserved buildings erected at the turn of the 19th and 20th centuries. These buildings, many resembling miniature palaces, were to become embassies, governmental departments or the offices of private companies. The three-storey house with a porch at No.49 is particularly worth seeing; it was built in 1833 and remodelled in the early 20th century. The eclecticist palace at No. 33, built in 1900 is now the Bulgarian Embassy while a Renaissance palace holds the Swiss Embassy. No. 12-14 is the Marconi family's palace which was formerly known as the Palace under the Artichoke, although the facade is in fact decorated with a stone pine cone. House No. 17, in the early modernist style, was constructed for the tradesman Michał Szlechow who imported exclusive Astrahan caviar. It is now a pharmacy. House No.19 has modernist decoration and was built for H Kolberg, a producer of optical devices. The interiors are sumptious, with neo-baroque boudoirs and white marble fireplaces direct from Paris.

Ujazdowski Palace

This early-baroque castle was built between 1619-20 on the scarp above the Piaseczyński channel, eventually becoming the king's summer residence. The kings of the Wettin dynasty hunted

Historical houses on Ujazdowskie Avenue

animals brought from Lithuania to the neighbouring woods. The castle was plundered in 1655 by the Swedish army and subsequently remodelled in 1690. During a later reconstruction two wings were added and the palace was turned into a barracks and also served as a military hospital. Burnt to the ground in 1939, it was rebuilt in 1954 and in 1970 was changed again, this time into a two-storey square castle with four towers and an internal courtyard. At present it holds the Modern Art Centre (*Centrum Sztuki Współczesnej*), a cinema, a restaurant and a café.

Address: Aleje Ujazdowskie 6

Obserwatorium Astronomiczne (Astronomical Observatory)

This piece of equipment was built for Warsaw University in the neo-Renaissance style between 1820 and 1824, and in the 19th century its highest terrace also served as an observation platform for the botanical garden as well as being an attraction in its own right. The building was burned during the Warsaw Uprising and reconstructed in 1948-49.

Address: Aleje Ujazdowskie 4

The monument to Marshal Józef Piłsudski

The Monument to King John III Sobieski

This baroque monument by André Le Brun was set by King Stanislaus Augustus Poniatowski in 1788 on the Agricola Bridge. The monument shows King John III Sobieski, a national hero as a result of the 17th-century wars with Turkey, in full armour on a rearing horse, before him a beaten Turk. The monument is clearly visible from the windows of the Palace on the Water (*Pałac na Wodzie*).

Łazienki Królewskie (Royal Łazienki Park)

Łazienki is a 73ha park containing a number of unusual attractions. The park blends the harmonious French style with the English in its reference to wild landscapes. The parks most precious trees are the two 300-year-old English oaks and the beeches (see *Walk: The Łazienkowski Garden* p96), and it is also filled with fragrant bushes and flowers. The park owes its shape to King Stanislaus Augustus Poniatowski, who bought it in the second half of the 18th century and had its geometric layout created.

Belweder Palace

At the end of the Ujazdowskie Avenues, right next to Łazienki Park, is the white palace called the Belweder. This is a baroque palace dating from the first half of the 18th century, which was bought and incorporated into the Łazienki complex by King Stanislaus Augustus Poniatowski. In an outbuilding the king established a factory of china and faience

The Astronomical Observatory

Piłsudski mementoes, and The Order of the Virtuti Militari Rooms (*Gabinety Orderu Virtuti Militari*). A monument to Piłsudski is located near the entrance to Łazienki Gardens.

Address: Belwederska 52

Józef Piłsudski

Józef Piłsudski (1867-1935) was a Polish marshal, the founder of the Polish Legions and the commander of their renowned First Brigade, as well as the political leader of a Poland reborn after 123 years of foreign domination. He is undoubtedly the most notable Polish politician of the 20th century. He held the title of Temporal Head of Poland in 1918, in 1919-20 was full Head of Poland and after 1920 he was simply the Marshal. He commanded the Polish army during the Polish-Bolshevik war of 1919-20 and at the Battle of Warsaw, also known as the Miracle on the Vistula, he outflanked the Soviet Red Army to win a stunning and overwhelming victory, successfully defending Warsaw and arguably the whole of Europe. In May 1926 he instigated the regime named *Sanacja* (national healing) and was Prime Minister in the years 1926-28. In 1930 he took the role of general inspector of the Polish army. He died of stomach cancer in 1935 and was buried in Cracow's Wawel Castle in a crypt beneath the Silver Bells Tower.

(glazed earthenware pots) also named Belweder, the finished products known as *belwedery*.

On the nights of 28th-30th November 1830, a group of conspirators attacked the Russian tsar's governor, Prince Constantine who was living at the palace, thus beginning the November Uprising. The prince escaped dressed as a woman. In 1919 the palace was home to Marshal Józef Piłsudski and then became the residence of Polish Presidents. Visitors to the palace may see the exhibition entitled *Józef Piłsudski*, which is home to

Parks and Palaces

Finding a peaceful spot in this busy metropolis is a simple
matter. Warsaw is known for its park and garden complexes
and its small green squares which provide rest and shade on
hot days. Another attraction is the extensive woodlands such
as Kabacki forest *(Las Kabacki)* and Powsin located close to
the southern edge of the city. Kampinoski National Park and
its woodlands lie to the north.

A peacock - the jewel of
Łazienkowski Park

The longest green area in the centre is that
on the eastern side of Ujazdowskie
Avenue: the Ujazdowski *(Park Ujazdowski)*
Agricola and Royal Łazienki Parks.
Ujazdowski Park begins in Piękna Street
and at the turn of the 19th century was the
site of agricultural fairs, public
entertainments and military parades. In
1896 the park was converted into the
regular park which exists today. A little
below Ujazdowski Castle is Agricola Park
which was designed for sports and
recreation. It is also a meeting place for the
young and often serves as a stage for
outdoor performances. The line of parks
along Ujazdowskie Avenue ends with the
most remarkable, Royal Łazienki (see *Walk:
The Łazienkowski Garden* p96).

In the early 19th century Warsaw
University's botanical garden was laid out
on land removed from the Łazienki Garden
and at around the same time the
Astronomical Observatory was established
in its twin-towered classical building. The
observatory, built over the period 1819-25
and faithfully reconstructed after the
Second World War, stands beside the

hothouse. However, much more valuable
scientifically is the botanical garden located
in Powsin, not far from Wilanów.

Mokotowskie Fields *(Pola Mokotowskie)*
are a favourite with the young. They are
the site of Warsaw's first airport, from
where the 2200m^3 hot-air balloons set off in
the Gordon Bennett Cup. When the airport
was moved to Okęcie it was suggested that
elegant blocks of flats be built here, yet the
plans were never realised due to the
outbreak of the Second World War. Now
the fields are full of cyclists and roller-
bladers riding the prepared tracks. There
are huge lawns, pubs which open until late
at night and a pond.

The most attractive park is the Saski
Garden which is located in the city centre
between Marszałkowska and Królewska
Streets and Piłsudskiego Square. With its
antique figures and 19th-century
architecture it is a favourite haunt of the
upper and middle classes, the old chestnut
trees providing protection from the summer
sun. It is also popular with families,
perhaps for the ducks patrolling the pond.

At Wilanów, close to the palace, there

was once a geometrical, clipped garden modelled on that at Versailles in France; however, this has since been transformed into a romantic and almost wild park in the English style which rambles on as far as the Vistula's old bed.

The park behind Krasiński Palace, designed by Tylman van Gameren, has been transformed to an even greater extent. At the turn of the 18th and 19th centuries this was a fashionable spot for meeting and walking; unfortunately, nothing has survived to the present day except the gates with their mascarons.

On Warsaw's right bank are two parks, Praski and Skaryszewski. Praski Park is located near the Śląsko-Dąbrowski Bridge *(Most Śląsko-Dąbrowski)* and replaced the ruins of Napoleonic fortifications. Now it is part of the zoo. Skaryszewski Park, near the Washington Roundabout *(Rondo Waszyngtona),* is located partially over the 11th-century settlement of Kamionki. The lake in the park reflects this, bearing the name *Jeziorko Kamionkowskie.*

Warsaw possesses completely new gardens too, for example those located on the roofs of the University Library where the upper and lower parts are even joined by a stream. These gardens are a favourite place for students and local people alike to take a walk (see *The City's Modern Architecture* p60-1).

The modern garden of the University Library

Walk: Łazienkowski Garden

The unique atmosphere of Royal Łazienki is conjured up by the Theatre on the Island and the Palace on the Water, as well as by romantic cafés and avenues. This beautiful example of an 18th-century complex of architecture and greenery pulses with life year-round: in spring it is visited by lovers of the rebirth of nature; in summer it becomes a place of rest for families; the golden autumn attracts those smitten by rich hues; in winter the museums, restaurants and cafés fill up.

Allow 2 hours.

1 The Monument to Frederyk Chopin

A widely-recognised symbol of Warsaw, this Secession (Art Nouveau movement)

The monument to Frederyk Chopin

monument was designed by Wacław Szymanowski in the early 20th century and placed in Łazienki in 1926. During the Second World War it was completely destroyed, but after a successful reconstruction based on old models and photographs it was returned to its miraculously-saved plinth in 1958. From spring until autumn the stage by the monument hosts concerts of Chopin's music.

2 Świątynia Sybilli (Sybilla's Temple)

Built of timber in the classical style in about 1820, this building makes reference to the antique Greek temples.

3 Wodozbiór (The Water Collector)

Near the Old Orangery is a small round building with an internal courtyard, modelled on the tomb of Cecilia Matteli in Via Apia in Rome. Here rain water was once collected and piped to the park fountains, although art exhibitions are now organised here and stalls with amber products stand nearby.

4 Stara Pomarańczarnia (Old Orangery)

Picturesquely located at the foot of the scarp, the southern wing of this 18th-century orangery holds a tree collection, while the eastern is home to the famous Stanisławowski Theatre built in 1774-77. The Stanisławowski Theatre is a rare example of a well-preserved 18th-century court theatre. Worth seeing are the paintings by Plerch of *Apollo's quadriga* with illusionistic paintings presenting the audience from the times of the reign of King Stanislaus Augustus Poniatowski. The Old Orangery also hosts the Gallery of Polish Sculpture *(Galeria Rzeźby Polskiej)* with its collection of antique marble and gypsum sculptures collected by Stanislaus Augustus Poniatowski for his planned Academy of Fine Art.

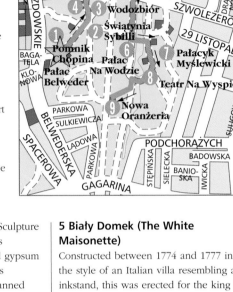

5 Biały Domek (The White Maisonette)

Constructed between 1774 and 1777 in the style of an Italian villa resembling an inkstand, this was erected for the king to entertain his mistresses. The maisonette was home to Louis XVIII, King of France, for the whole of his time in Poland in 1801.

6 Pałac Na Wodzie (Palace on the Water)

In medieval times this area was covered with forest and belonged to the Dukes of Mazovia who used it as a hunting ground for the *aurochs* (extinct wild ox) which inhabited the woods, but in 1674 it was taken over by Marshal Lubomirski, who decided to change its character. The Dutch architect Tylman van Gameren

A sundial in Lazieki Park

designed the hermitage with the bathroom (*łazienka*) which gave the park its name. In the years 1772-93 D Merlini profoundly remodelled Lubomirski's bathroom as a summer residence for the kings and in this way the Palace on the Water was created, the most prominent example of Polish 18th-century classical architecture. The decoration with baroque elements was performed by J C Kamsetzer with the painters M Bacciarelli and J B Plerch, as well as by numerous sculptors and stucco artists. The demolished palace was reconstructed after World War II and all of the art collections belonging to Stanislaus Augustus Poniatowski were returned.

Since 1960 the palace has been a branch of the National Museum. The Ballroom (*Sala Balowa*), Bachus room and bathroom with its Dutch tiles are all worthy of a visit. The royal apartments were also reconstructed, the original items being the king's table and bed. The Thursday Dinner Hall (*Sala Obiadów Czwartkowych*) is home to an 18th-century bust of the king and the sculpture

The New Orangery in its picturesque setting

of Hebe, the Greek goddess of youth. After a tour the Trou Madame café, located near the palace, is recommended for its coffee.

7 Myślewicki Palace and the Great Outbuilding

This palace was built in 1775-84 in the village of Myślewice for Stanislaus Augustus Poniatowski's nephew, prince Józef Poniatowski. The palace also housed a military school, students of which attacked the Belweder palace in November 1830, beginning the November Uprising. Now the palace serves as the Ignacy Paderewski Museum and the Museum of Polish Emigration (*Muzeum Polskiego Wychodźctwa*). The Great Outbuilding was constructed for royal servants in 1788.

8 Teatr na Wyspie (Theatre on the Island)

The theatre is in fact an amphitheatre with a stage designed by the prolific J C Kamsetzer in 1790-91. The

The Thursday Dinner Room in the Palace on the Water

The Theatre on the Island, modelled on the Herculanum theatre

rounded auditorium was modelled on antique theatres, with decorations imitating the ruins of the Temple of Jupiter in Baalbeck in Syria. The stage and auditorium are separated by water, allowing boats to be moored for performances. In September 1791, to celebrate the election of Stanislaus Augustus Poniatowski, *Cleopatra* was staged, the actors afloat. Plays are still performed here in the summer. After visiting the theatre the *Amfiteatr* winery is a suitable next destination.

9 Nowa Oranżeria (New Orangery)

The cast-iron and glass New Orangery was built in 1860-61 and amongst its tropical vegetation Warsaw's most expensive restaurant may be found, *Belvedere*. This restaurant has hosted Queen Elizabeth II, the former German Chancellor Helmut Kohl and the former First Lady of the United States, Hilary Clinton, and the venue offers a romantic candlelit atmosphere.

Thursday Dinners

The old dining room of the Palace on the Water is also known as the Thursday Dinner Room, as on Thursdays King Stanislaus Augustus Poniatowski invited artists and writers to dine with him. The dinners were organised between 1771 and 1782, in winter the whole party moving to the Marble Hall at the Royal Castle. The king was entertained with dessert by means of jokes and short obscene lyrics printed on papers slipped under the places around the table. The leading jokers were the writer and bishop Ignacy Krasicki and the court poet Adam Naruszewicz. There were also serious discussions on politics, literature and art and the dessert that traditionally concluded the proceedings was plums.

Museums and Galleries

The majority of Warsaw's numerous museums and galleries will repay any interest shown them. The richest of the collections is undoubtedly that possessed by the National Museum, which, besides the works of Polish artists, contains paintings by the greatest European painters. Botticelli's *Madonna with Child* and Bardone's *Venus and Amor* are gems of the collection, while the collection of Frescoes from Faras is also worth seeing.

The staircase of the Zachęta Gallery

Several precious works by both Polish and foreign artists are also held at the Royal Castle, the most precious being *Portrait of the Scholar* by Rembrandt, the gift of Professor Karolina Lankorońska.

Interesting collections are on show at the Ethnographic Museum *(Museum Etnograficzne)*, the Museum of Technology *(Muzeum Techniki)*, the Poster Museum *(Muzeum Plakatu)* and the Museum of the Polish Army *(Muzeum Wojska Polskiego)*. Contemporary art is exhibited at the Modern Art Centre *(Centrum Sztuki Współczesnej)* and Zachęta Gallery, while works both old and new from the lands of Asia and the Pacific may be seen at the Museum of Asia and the Pacific *(Muzeum Azji i Pacyfiku)*.

Centrum Sztuki Współczesnej (Modern Art Centre)

Founded in early 1980s at the reconstructed Ujazdowski Castle *(see Aleje Ujazdowskie p88-93)*, the Modern Art Centre comprises several temporary exhibitions, cinemas, a library and a modern art information centre. The gallery

organises exhibitions of the most famous artists from all over the world and visitors are welcome in the castle's café and restaurant Qchnia Artystyczna.
Address: Aleje Ujazdowskie 6

Galeria Zachęta (Zachęta Gallery)

The Society of Fine Art, along with this its gallery, was founded in 1860 by artists and art lovers, with the gallery located in a building designed by Stefan Szyller from

The exhibition *Everything is OK* by Jarosław Fliciński at the Modern Art Centre

1899 to 1903. The main purpose of the society was to promote Polish art and to this end it organised exhibitions, annual art 'parlours', sales and lotteries, and also bought works of art. In 1990 the society bought *The Battle of Grunwald* by Matejko, *Hunting with Greyhounds* by Chełmoński and *Two Heads* by Malczewski as well as many other paintings by Wyspiański, Pankiewicz and the Gierymski brothers. On 16th December 1922 *Zachęta* witnessed a tragic event, the assassination of President Gabriel Narutowcz by the mentally-ill painter Eligiusz Niewiadomski.

The building housing *Zachęta,* with its classical facade in the academic Renaissance, survived the Second World War and in 1955 had a fourth wing added in accordance with the original architectural plans. In the 1950s the gallery's collections were moved to the National Museum and *Zachęta* became a place of temporary exhibitions. Besides modern art, there are interesting review exhibitions covering such things as the development of Polish art set against the background of international trends, the works of Polish artists overseas and those of illustrious European artists. In addition, the popular *World Press Photo* event is held here.
Address: Plac Małachowskiego 3

Muzeum Archeologiczne (Archeological Museum)

The Archeological Museum is housed in the historical Arsenal, which was built in 1643 by King Ladislas IV Vasa as an element of Warsaw's fortifications. Many exhibits date from the neolithic period and come from Poland, wider Europe, Asia,

A part of the exhibition *Last Supper* by Andriej Filpow

America and Africa, but other exhibitions are entitled *The Prehistory of the Polish Lands, The ABC of Romanesque Architecture* and *The Alphabet of Gothic Architecture*. The museum also provides special classes teaching visitors to weave colourful ribbons, make pottery using traditional techniques and produce glass jewellery according to old designs.
Address: Długa 52

Muzeum Azji i Pacyfiku (Museum of Asia and the Pacific)

This museum was opened in 1976 and has two galleries. The first called *Nusantra* is located on Nowogrodzka Street, the second called the Asian *(Azjatycka)* is to be found on Freta Street. The founder of the institution was the collector and Asian art enthusiast Andrzej

The Museum of Asia and the Pacific

Wawrzyniak, who displayed his collection of 3,000 items here. In addition, in the late 1970s the museum received numerous valuable exhibits such as Buddha statues dating from the 6th century BC, from the earliest days of Buddhism. Both galleries organise temporary exhibitions devoted to the culture and art of Asian countries.
Address: Galera Azjatycka – Freta 6, Nusantara – Nowogrodzka 18a

Museum Etnograficzne (Ethnographic Museum)

Located in a neo-renaissance building designed by E Marconi, the Ethnographic Museum exhibits Polish folk costumes, folk art and crafts and old customs, as well as ethnographic collections from Africa, Australia, Oceania and Latin and South America. Temporary exhibitions are also organised. The museum is also concerned with scientific research into costumes, lace, embroidery, folk painting, graphics, cutouts and sculpture.

Part of an exhibition at the Ethnographic Museum

Address: Kredytowa 1

Muzeum Karykatury (Museum of Caricature)

The Gardener's House *(Dom Ogrodnika)* at the Primate's Palace *(see Palaces p76-81)* is the home of this museum which was founded in 1978 by the master of Polish caricature, Eryk Lipiński. He gifted his own collection of caricatures and archive to the museum. The collection consists of drawings, portraits and engravings as well as magazines from all over the world. The museum organises frequently-changing temporary exhibitions of both Polish and foreign works in two halls.

Address: Kozia 11

Muzeum Narodowe (National Museum)

Founded in 1862 as the Museum of Fine Art this institution has, since 1916, become known as the National Museum. The museum received its own building in 1938 when the construction of Tadeusz Tołwiński's modernist design was completed, and from 1965 to 1972 additional sections were added facing the park. Containing antique and medieval items, the collection was established in the years 1926-38, although the unique collection of Christian frescoes from Faras in Sudan was added in 1972. The frescoes were discovered by a Polish archeologist working under the guidance of Professor Kazimierz Michałowski and had been painted between the 7th and 9th centuries in the cathedral in Nubia, a seat of Christian bishops. This collection includes excellent representations of St Anna, St Peter the Apostle, St Paul the Evangelist

Ujazdowski Castle, home of the Modern Art Centre

and the bishop from Faras named Petros who commissioned the paintings. The gallery devoted to contemporary and modern art possesses works of the Italian, French, Dutch, German and Flamande schools, all of interest to art lovers. This gallery displays works by Botticelli, Cranach and Brueghel Senior. The gallery of contemporary art displays work by Corbet, Vlamnick and Signac. Polish paintings and modern art are hung in the medieval gallery. A place of especial interest is the Polish art gallery and Polish modern art gallery where the most famous national works are gathered; those of Matejko, Michałowski, Rodakowski, Wyspiański, Wyczółkowski and Maleczewski. Polish painting and sculpture from the pre-war period are also represented.

Address: Aleje Jerozolimskie 3

Muzeum Plakatu w Wilanowie (Poster Museum at Wilanów)

The Poster Museum, a branch of the National Museum, was opened at Wilanów in 1968 in exhibition halls converted from the old stables and carriage shed. The museum is home to one of the world's largest collections of artistic posters, one which includes 30,000 Polish posters and 20,000 foreign, among them the work of Andy Warhol. The museum also organises annual reviews and the *International Poster Biennale*.

Address: Stanisława Kostki Potockiego 10/16

Muzeum Techniki NOT (Museum of Technology)

This museum is to be found in the Palace of Culture and Science, built from 1952 to 55. The museum's collection is subdivided into the categories *Communication and Transport, Mining and Metallurgy, Farming, Forestry, The Wood Industry, The Food Industry, The Basis of Technology, Teletechnology, Astronautics* and *Atomics*. Exhibitions also present an interesting collection of old cars and motorcycles, gramophones and the world-famous Enigma encryption machine that cracked German codes during the Second World War. Visitors to the planetarium may admire the stars and shining replica spacecraft. Beyond this, the museum's temporary exhibitions showcase the work of Polish collectors, such as those of toy cars, twenty-year-old electronics and suchlike.

Address: Pałac Kultury i Nauki. Defilad Square. Entrance from the side of al. Jerozolimskie.

Muzeum Wojska Polskiego (Museum of the Polish Army)

Marshal Józef Piłsudski founded this museum by decree in 1920, although its present location dates from 1933. The museum houses the country's largest collection of militaria, covering the history of the Polish army from medieval times to the end of the Second World War. The oldest exhibit is a gold helmet *(szyszak)* from the time of the first Christian kings.

Of particular interest is the 17th-century armour of winged *Husaria* cavalry decorated with eagle feathers and leopard skins to terrify the enemy, one exhibit showing a warrior astride a horse. The *Husaria* contributed to victory at Vienna in 1683 and the battles in eastern Poland. Other exhibits from these times include rich ornamentation of armour and the tent of a Turkish commander, while the museum also possesses uniforms of all military formations and banners, accessories, maps, medals and photographs. The collection is rounded off with weaponry from

Armour from the Museum of the Polish Army

The Arrival of the Legions in Warsaw, by Stanisław Bagiński at the Museum of the Polish Army

other European countries, as well as from Asia, Africa and Australia. The park surrounding the museum is scattered with old tanks, aircraft and artillery pieces.
Address: Aleje Jerozolimskie 3

Muzeum Ziemi (Earth Museum)

The Earth Museum is located across two buildings, the first is the old Branicki Palace, rebuilt in classical form in 1948 after the Second World War, the second is a villa designed in 1781. The museum's collection contains 150,000 rock and mineral samples as well as irregular stones of imposing dimensions, palaeontological finds and one of the world's largest collections of amber.
Address: Aleje Na Skarpie 20/26 and 27

The Warsaw Historical Museum

(see Walk: Around the Old Town Market Square p38)

The Adam Mickiewicz Museum of Literature

(see Walk: Around the Old Town Market Square p38)

The Maria Skłodowska-Curie Museum

(see Walk: Around the New Town Market Square p48)

The Museum of the Warsaw

(see Warsaw Uprising p14-5)

The Royal Castle

(see The Royal Castle p42-3)

Monuments

Since time immemorial Varsovians have commemorated the meritorious citizens of Poland and its capital with monuments. The first was the Column of King Sigismund III Vasa, erected in 1644, but the city also remembers the thousands killed fighting occupiers and those who were murdered, on stones and commemorative tablets embedded in the squares, parks and streets. Writers, musicians and politicians are also sculpted standing or sitting, among them the poet Adam Mickiewicz.

Monument to Prus, on Krakowskie Przedmieście

Perhaps the most well-known Varsovian monument of all though is the Mermaid. This beautiful woman, created by K Hegel in 1855, with her long fish tail holds a sword and a shield and stands on the Old Market Square.

Another Mermaid monument was created in bronze by Nitschowa before the Second World War, her face bestowed by the young poet Krystyna Krahelska who was killed during the Warsaw Uprising. The bronze maiden survived the war and, owing to her watery associations, now stands by the Vistula near Świętokrzyski Bridge.

One of the best monuments is that to Copernicus which was sculpted by Berthel Thorvaldsen and ordered at the time of the construction of the Warsaw Scientific Society's seat. Warsaw had been waiting for the monument for 10 years and the wait was certainly worth it. The classical monument with

its simplicity of form and evident symbolism suits Staszic's Palace well.

Thorvaldsen's hands also sculpted the monument to Prince Józef Poniatowski. The gypsum 'Prince Pepi', as Poniatowski's statue was nicknamed, arrived in Warsaw shortly before the November Uprising, and after the Uprising's failure the Russian tsar ordered the monument to be melted down. Fortunately, the tsar's general took a liking to the monument and took it for his house in Gomel. Prince Pepi finally returned to his newly-independent homeland in 1923 and now sits on horseback in front of the Presidential Palace.

Warsaw preferred not to set statues of its kings on plinths, not withstanding two notable exceptions. One of these was made for King Sigismund III Vasa who stands on Zamkowy Square. The second was made for the monument to King John III Sobieski near Agricola who is seen trampling a Turk.

This sandstone monument was unveiled on the 105th anniversary of his victory at Vienna on 14th September 1788.

Monuments to writers and musicians are often encountered on the city's squares. The chronicler of Warsaw, the writer Prus, seems to be crossing the square not far from the Bristol Hotel, slightly bent over his stick. Maria Konopnicka, author of numerous works for children, may be found in the Saski Gardens, which are visited by mothers with children. The fathers of the Polish stage, Moniuszko and Bogusławski, stand in front of the Great Theatre, while the romantic poet Słowacki stands on Bankowy Square.

The greatest number of monuments are devoted to the heroes of Warsaw's history. Stretching across Grójecks Street is a peculiar monument, one in the form of a date 8th-17th September 1939. It stands on the site of the barricade which at the outset of the Second World War held out the longest of all.

Varsovians have waited a long time for a matronly monument to the insurgents of the city. The first monument, built in 1964, was an expressive sculpture liked by Varsovians but deemed unsatisfactory; its sword-bearing female figure called Warsaw's *Nike* was only symbolic and said too little. Then in 1989, the long-expected monument to the 1944 Warsaw Uprising was unveiled on Krasicki Square. In this, one group of rebels of unnatural height appears to be fighting, while a second seems to be descending into the sewer system. Teenage heroes were commemorated by the *Monument to the Little Insurgent*, this figure of a young boy with a helmet too big for him and a machine gun in hands located next to the Old Town's defensive walls. More monuments, stones and tablets commemorate the victims of totalitarianism, the murdered and the executed. Such an emphatic monument stands on Stawki Street, depicting a railway goods wagon with a cluster of crosses atop. This commemorates the exiles from Poland's eastern territories who were transferred to Siberia and persecuted by Stalin.

The monument to Copernicus in front of S Staszic's Palace

Along Marszałkowskiej Street

The history of this street is not a long one. Its first stretch was built in the 18th century and it rose to the status of the main route in the 19th, when the bulk of the city's traffic concentrated along it. Before the Second World War it was the city's busiest street. There were hundreds of shops, restaurants, cafés and bars here, several schools, eight cinemas, a number of banks and richly-decorated houses occupied by Warsaw's intellectuals.

The early 20th-century House under the Eagles

Around Bankowy Square

What is currently Marszałkowska Street began at Bankowy Square. The street's course dates to the 19th century and was affected during the years 1876–78 when the engineer Linley was setting out the city's sewer system. He wished to cross the area of Saski Park with his pipes yet when local residents opposed his plans the Russian general and Mayor of Warsaw had to promise that the park would not suffer a loss of territory. This is why, today this generally straight street curves a little near the Saski Gardens.

Marszałkowska Street leads on to the junction with Królewska Street, which itself runs to the *Zachęta* Gallery and Małachowskiego Square. This is the central part of the old Małachowski *jurydyka,* a private territory independent of municipal and judicial authority and the site of the rotund Protestant-Lutheran Church of the Holy Trinity, which is covered by a green dome and resembles the Roman Pantheon. The church burnt down in 1939 but was quickly rebuilt following the Second World War and now has excellent acoustics, the reason that music lovers attend the concerts held there.

In Kredytowa Street, which borders Małachowski Square to the south is the Ethnographic Museum, the building of which was designed by Marconi and modelled on the Venetian Sansovino's Library.

Pałac Kultury i Nauki (Palace of Culture and Science)

The Palace of Culture and Science is located on Parade Square *(pl.Defilad)* which adjoins Marszałkowska Street. The palace's most attractive room is the Congress Hall *(Sala Kongresowa),* which hosts renonwed artists as well as festivals such as the *Jazz Jamboree*.

Today the palace is home to museums of technology and palaeontology, the theatres *Studio, Dramatyczny* and *Lalka,* the Youth Centre, an indoor swimming pool and a bank, not to mention cafés and restaurants. The palace's halls are also hired for exhibitions and trade fairs, while the top floor accommodates the Polish Academy of Science, Warsaw University and Warsaw's Municipal Office. On the 30th floor there is a viewing terrace.

Around the Eastern Wall

The Eastern Wall is a complex of shopping malls, blocks of flats and offices. Pre-war Warsaw does not exist on this stretch of Marszałkowska Street, and the hinterland of the Eastern Wall is covered with skyscrapers and block of flats. For more historical sites a walk to the area of S Moniuszki, Sienkiewicza and Jasna Streets is recommended. Here the seat of the National Philharmonic may be seen which is modelled on the Paris Opera House and

A busy passage between shopping centres

is where, on 5th November 1905, the genius pianist Ignacy Jan Paderewski participated in the inauguration ceremony, the man who was later to become the first Prime Minister of the independent Poland.

The classical buildings erected after the Second World War are less decorative with fewer ornate ceilings, sculptures and gilded elements. The National Philharmonic hosts the most important musical events in Poland, for example the finals of the *F Chopin International Piano Contest*. Close by at No.8 Moniuszki Street is the pre-war home of the Italian Adria Insurance Society, today of PZU, which had an elegant eating establishment on the ground floor where the entire pre-war cream of society entertained. On the corner of Jasna Street is the interesting building of the Cooperative Bank, dated 1912-17, which is also known as the 'House under the Eagles', after the eagles at the corners. It is modern, an excellent example of modernist architecture.

Powstańców Warszawy Square may be reached via the short Przeskok Street. From the south the square is bordered by

Colourful stained-glass window in the Jabłkowski Brothers' Shopping Centre

the next few floors is a large bookshop and on the top floor is a café where meetings with authors are organised – culture and commerce coming together.

Jerozolimskie Avenue

At the junction of Marszałkowska Street and Jerozolimskie Avenue is a stone signpost bearing distances to major European cities. The facades of Jerozolimskie Avenue are typical of the Secession style, with one of the most attractive buildings being the *Polonia* hotel which dates from early 20th century and is beautifully illuminated at dusk.

The house at No.51 Jerozolimskie Avenue is home to a fascinating item, a photo-plasticon ('living picture' machines invented in the 19th century), the sole example in the world and one still possessed by the same family, the Chudys. The slide barrel is operated by Tadeusz Chudy, the son of Taduesz Senior and the grandson of Józef Chudy, Józef having done the same long before the Second World War. Three-dimensional slides of old Warsaw and exotic lands can be seen, and sitting in the dark at the wooden barrel peering through the viewer is good fun. *(Before visiting, it is necessary to call the owner on +48 22 625 35 52.)*

In the area of Nowogrodzka Street, which is perpendicular to Marszałkowska Street and parallel to Jerozolimskie Avenue, few buildings from before the Second World War have survived although there is the pre-war Post Office building, *Roma* Musical Theatre and attractive

Szpitalna Street and on the corner of Szpitalna and Górskiego Street is an eclecticist building with elements of the French Renaissance style. The building is dated 1893 and was the property of the famous Wedel family, whose name was to become synonymous with chocolate production.

At the point where Szpitalna intersects Chmielna and Krucza Streets is the old Jabłkowski Brothers' Shopping Centre. Constructed in 1913-14 for trading, it miraculously survived the war together with its stained-glass windows. The cellars now hold a music shop while spread over

Agricultural Bank. Nowogrodzka Street has strong commercial traditions and in the 19th century the corner with Poznańska Street was the site of wool markets to which sheep breeders, mostly gentry, came to sell their wool to the city's merchants. The culminating day was 15th June when the capital was visited by crowds from the provinces. Nobles and their wives came to buy a number of things in the city and shops and restaurants were full. Shortly after the Second World War bazaars on Poznańska began again. The whole area is now built up with governmental institutions and tenement buildings, while narrow-gauge WKD trains run in the street.

MDM

Heading further south, in the direction of Mokotów, the MDM quarter is encountered, built between 1952-55. It begins in Wilcza Street, where only a few houses survived the war, among them a neo-Gothic house built from clinker bricks with ogival arches and a turret. No. 44 is a pre-war pharmacy which survived, even continuing to function without interruption.

The post-war town planners intended to make Marszałkowska Street the 'Champs-Elysées of Warsaw', the reason ruined houses were torn down and the street broadened from 27.5 to 60m. The wider Marszałkowska Street lost its bustling character yet preserved its commercial function, there still being plenty of shops, banks and estate and travel agencies. On the rectangular Konstytucji Square Marszałkowska Street is a broad thoroughfare, whereas a little further on it has shrunk to its pre-war dimensions. With

Part of the richly-decorated facade of the Polonia hotel

its stream of cars moving south, the now one-way Marszałkowska Street reaches Salvador Square *(Plac Zbawiciela)*.

Plac Zbawiciela / KościółNajświętszego Zbawiciela (Salvador Square / Holiest Salvador Church

Zbawiciela Square with its half-rounded collonade was planned in the 1760s, while the white body of the Holiest Salvador Church is clearly visible and was built at the beginning of the 20th century. This basilica was designed by Dziekoński, architect of several Mazovian churches, and is a good example of the fashionable national style which blends eclecticism with various elements of Polish architecture. The building has a shapely body, two slender towers with high crowns and rich decoration in its sculptures of St Peter and Paul.

Another interesting building is the mission of the American Methodists which from the darkest times of communism until today has been an excellent school of English. All of the city's post-war generations were taught the language of Shakespeare here.

Around the Technical University of Warsaw

The architecture of pre-war Warsaw has been preserved on two neighbouring squares, Konstytucji and Politechniki Warszawskiej. On the corner of Konstytucji Square and Koszykowa Street is the grey seat of the Department of Architecture, and a little further on is a building with interesting reliefs including the heads of

One of the few surviving neo-Gothic houses on Marszałkowska Street

Secession houses wow on Lwowska Street

angels, animals and people. Koszykowa Street leads to the Market Hall dating from the early 20th century, popularly known as *Koszyki*. Its secession and realistic decorations are clear to see. The walk under the MDM arcades from Waryńskiego Street to Lwowska, taking in early 20th-century modernist houses with secession decoration, is also worthwhile. The architecture on Śniadeckich Street has a similar character.

Lwowska Street leads to Politechniki Warszawskiej Square and the main building of Warsaw's Technical University, which is dated 1899-1901. The origins of this institution go back to the Polytechnic founded in 1825. The building blends Renaissance and baroque elements, with its high aulum surrounded by inner galleries and has a rich educational and political tradition.

Unii Lubelskiej Square

Behind Zbawiciela Square, Marszałkowska Street runs high above the Łazienkowska Route, directly to Unii Lubelskiej Square.

This stretch is uninteresting in terms of architecture, although Unii Lubelskiej Square itself is decorated with several interesting buildings, as are the neighbouring streets. On Bagatela Street which leads out of the square, the Polish poet Krzysztof Kamil Baczyński lived at house No.10. Sucha Avenue, running diagonally from the square, which took its name from King Stanislaus Augustus Poniatowski's gardener. Now the street has more sinister connotations as it was the site of Gestapo headquarters during the occupation. At present the headquarters building is in the possession of the Ministry of Education and Sport and it contains the Museum of Combat and Martyrdom commemorating the thousands of Polish patriots interrogated and beaten by the Gestapo. The small cream-coloured building is an old tollgate. Beyond the square the modern Puławska Financial Centre is visible.

An eclecticist building; the Technical University

In the first years after the Second World War the reconstruction of Warsaw was begun. The rubble and ruins were removed and on the cleared areas new quarters were built,

reconstruction based on pre-war projects by J Chmielewski and S Syrkus from 1934. The architectural trends from the 1930s were still alive - reserved forms of eclecticism, the so-called national style and moderate monumentalism. Functionalism gave birth in 1947 to the Central Shopping Centre, today's *Smyk*, which is simple but practical.

In 1949 Polish architecture returned to the fashionable concepts of national architecture. The Polish baroque and Renaissance were explored for inspiration, as was folk and regional architecture. Then the pretentious eclecticist style, full of unnecessary ornaments, columns, attics, reliefs and cartouches began to be formed. This was overpowering architecture on a huge scale and far removed from the needs of the ruined country. At that time all was required to be socialist and these concepts were embodied in the theory of social realism.

All new estates were designed this way, for instance Muranów, built on the ruins of the Jewish Ghetto in 1949-56. However, the best example is the MDM quarter (see p111), designed by the leading architects of the style. The spacial arrangement is typically baroque with the centre on Konstytucji Square, the columns around the square forming arcades with shops. Social-realist sculpture may not be a visual delight but it does have historical value, and the scenes on the reliefs here present the history of the MDM's creation. Despite the fame of the MDM's stone candlestick-like lamp-posts, the square has never had an aesthetic function. In fact, social-realism was criticised for its pomposity and falsehoods; the palatial houses are full of cage-like flats and badly-stocked shops were located under the arcades and between the columns.

The very essence of social-realist eclecticism is the Palace of Culture and Science (see p109) where the pseudo-

Gothic and pseudo-Renaissance body is enhanced by truly Soviet monumentalism and adorned with lamps, marble and of course columns. Sculptural decoration comes in the form of figures of people aware of

their functions and responsibilities in a socialist society. On the E Plater Street side the sculpture depicts cultural luminaries, while on the Marszałkowska Street side are those of the world of science.

The palace stands on Parade Square, the largest in Europe, but the plan to join this monument to social-realism with the tissue of the modern city awaits realisation. A multi-media Museum of Communism is planned, to be placed under Parade Square in front of the main entrance to the palace. This project requires no significant investment as the museum's halls will be located in basements joining the palace with the main tribune, from which communist leaders once made their speeches.

Far left: a demonstration by workers on a relief near Konstytucji Square
Left: the huge edifice of the Palace of Culture and Science
Above: Marszalkowska Street

The Area of the Former Ghetto

Inter-war Warsaw had the largest Jewish community in Europe. In 1938 about 375,000 Jews lived in the capital and this was 35 percent of the population, whereas on average about 8.5 percent of the remainder of Poland was Jewish. Varsovian Jews were incredibly dynamic and made an extraordinary contribution to the life and outlook of the city. Jewish education was developing, Jewish newspapers were published in both Polish and Yiddish and the Jewish theatre was in full bloom.

A granite block on the Passion Road

The Jewish community of the inter-war city fared extremely well. Jewish scientists gained international fame, while social leaders were influential. When a rabbi from Góra Kalwaria came into conflict with the director of Warsaw's WKD railway, the director went to the elderly man and apologised in person in order to avoid bankruptcy. In the first Polish Diet the Jewish party had 35 members while the first woman elected to the Polish parliament, Rosa Pomeranc-Melcer, was Jewish. Warsaw's Jewish community (cahal) managed hospitals, orphanages,

An archive photograph of the Great Synagogue

The classical facade of Mostowski Palace

sports clubs, cultural societies and cooperatives. The majority of Jews were members of the Varsovian working class, yet Jews were members of higher classes too. They were real, assimilated Varsovians: entrepreneurs, physicians, lawyers and bankers.

The poorer Jews occupied the so-called Northern Quarter, also in the majority in the districts of Muranów, Mirów, Powązki, Leszno and Grzybów and a significant number of Jews lived in the Old Town and parts of the city centre. Jews added colour to Dzielna, Pawia, Gęsia, Nalewki, Franciszkańska, Miła, Świętojerska and Muranowska Streets (many of which no

longer exist, or exist only partially). The courses of a number of such streets are revealed by tablets embedded in Parade Square.

Jewish Warsaw was overpopulated, busy and full of shops, small workshops and tavernas, as well as home to Orthodox Jews dressed in their long *chalat* and *jarmulcas*. Jews often carried their business with them in one bundle and, walking the streets, shouted invitations to look at the items they bore and to buy them. Danny, the main character of *The Magician from Lublin* by Nobel prize-winning author Izzak Singer, lived in such a world.

The impressive monument *Umschlagplatz* on Stawki Street

The city that disappeared

Almost nothing of the Northern Quarter survived as it was burned down in 1943 during the battle in the ghetto. The atmosphere of Jewish streets is conjured up in dilapidated yet surviving houses found on Próżna Street. Próżna Street is located near the Świętokrzyska underground station on Zielna Street and leads to Grzybowski Street. Here the ground floors are occupied by small shops where nails may be bought by the kilogram, as it was before the Second World War when the whole of Grzybowski Square was designated as the square of the metalware trade. At the *E Kamińska* Jewish Theatre plays in Yiddish are performed and excellent Jewish songs may sometimes be heard, while at the back of the theatre in Twarda Street is the Nożyks

Synagogue. It is still a Jewish temple but open to visitors on Thursdays. The entrance is modern and uninteresting but the building itself is authentic with neo-Romanesque and byzantine elements. There is a special balcony for women and a centrally-located *bima,* a special pedestal where the Torah scrolls are placed while they are read.

Grzybowski Square, the market square of the old Grzybów *jurydyka,* is dominated by the All Saints Church of E Marconi, which was completed at the beginning of the 20th century, despite its construction having started long before in 1868. It has two towers, rich sculptural ornamentation and a huge flight of steps leading to the entrance beneath a portico. Despite war damage, some original paintings have survived, for example

Crucifixion by Trevisani above the high altar and *Resurrection* by Siemiradzki.

At the end of the 19th century the Jewish synagogue was located on the site of the present Business Centre Club, yet this huge building now stands opposite the Saski Gardens between modern blocks of flats. This building is one of those which had to be moved from one place to another, another being the Church of the Nativity of the Holy Mother on Solidarności Avenue, which was moved about 21m to allow the widening of the street. The same reason led to Lubomirski Palace being moved just 1.8m and rotated 78 degrees to make way for Żelazna Brama Square. This square was occupied in the 19th century by a huge trade hall, yet today it is almost empty. The stone palace guarded by lions was built by Duke Radziwiłłin the 18th century and later rebuilt in the classical style. The front colonnade with ten Ionian columns was claimed to be the most imposing in the city but this changed when the Great Theatre was built. The palace was bought by the Jewish businessmen S Cohen and I Blass from Góra Kalwaria and served as a synagogue until the end of the 20th century

Beyond the Wielopole market hall in a westerly direction, the neo-Romanesque Mirowskie market halls were built between 1899-1901. They survived the war and today are full of shops, stalls and

A stone on the Bunker Monument

close to an outdoor market in the adjacent Elektoralna Street and Jana Pawła II Avenue.

The borders of the Jewish Ghetto ran along Wielka, Bagno, Grzybowski Square, Rynkowa, Zimna, Elektoralna, Plac Bankowy, Rymarska, Tłomackie, Przejazd, Ogród Krasińskich, Freta, Sapieżyńska, Konwiktorska, Stawki, Okopowa, Towatora, Srebrna and Złota. It was divided into two parts, the Large Ghetto and the Small Ghetto, which were joined by a wooden bridge. The Museum of the Holocaust in New York contains a replica of this bridge.

The wide artery of Jana Pawła II Avenue leads to Anielewicza Street and by turning left here the visitor may find Smocza Street, home to a restaurant offering Jewish cuisine. By turning right off Jana Pawła II Avenue, visitors arrive instead at a large square with a monument to the Heroes of the Ghetto (see *Walk: The Passion Road and the Fight of the Jews p122-3)*. On Zamenhofa Street adjoining the square was the house of the Jewish scholar who invented the language *Esperant* who lived and worked here between 1898 and 1915. Unfortunately the house has been replaced by a new one, but L Zamenhof is honoured by means of a plaque. Zamenhof Street leads to Andersa Street and by way of Mostowski Palace to Bankowy Square. Mostowski Palace with its internal courtyard has harboured national security institutions for a long time although the first owner organised much-appreciated literary discussions. Behind the palace is the *Muranów* cinema, in front of which stands a cast-iron fountain dated 1866 with a sculpture by Marconi. The roof of the cinema forms a terrace accessible to visitors who may look out over the Muranów quarter. This post-war quarter was built of crushed bricks from the ghetto on an uncleared area, the reason its buildings stand higher. This elevated area may be reached from the cinema's roof terrace via an arched gate.

On the eastern flank of Bankowy square is Tłomackie Street where the capital's largest synagogue was located. It was blown up by the Germans in 1943 who declared this barbaric act to be an 'unforgettable allegorical triumph over Jews'. The Old Synagogue was replaced by the Azure Tower in the 1970s. Not far away is the Jewish History Institute with its rich archives and library, which before the Second World War was the Judaic Science Institute. A piece of column from the Great Synagogue is stored here and the collection of old manuscripts is particularly precious. Those interested in Jewish matters may find the institute to be a valuable resource.

Aleja Solidarności leads to Okopowa Street, where the Jewish Cemetery is

Gravestones at the Jewish Cemetery

located. This old necropolis dates from 1906 and possesses the graves of several people associated with Polish culture and science, for example L Zamenhof, the creator of the most successful artificial language, Peret, a writer working in Yiddish, the mother of the Hollywood musician Jerzy Petersburski, famous for the Donna Clara tango, and Aleksander Hertz, the director who launched the actress Pola Negri. The cemetery is surrounded by a wall with embedded epitaphs. Jews were buried in a strict order in *macewa* (simple graves), rabbis were burned in *obele*.

There is also a symbolic place devoted to the heroes of the Ghetto Uprising and a monument to Dr Janusz Korczak and the Children of the Holocaust. Dr Korczak was a guardian of children at an orphanage

Polish and Hebrew inscriptions on the Monument to the Three Hundred Killed near the Cemetery

who voluntarily went with them to the concentration camp when the Nazis, who had intensified the transfer of Jews to the gas chambers in Treblinka, fixed 6th August 1942 as the date of a transfer of children. In 1942 everyone in the ghetto knew where and how the journey in the cattle wagon ended. Hasidic Jews dressed in the white skirts of death for this final journey.

The cemetery is a good place to consider the history of Jewish martyrdom. The majority of monuments are located in the post-war Muranów district, on Okopowa Street, on the district's main artery, Jana Pawła II Avenue, and near the Radosława roundabout.

Monument to heroes of the ghetto

The Warsaw Ghetto Uprising

The Warsaw Ghetto was created in 1940, around 180,000 Jews being forced to move inside. The area was surrounded by a 16km long and 3m high wall which sealed off what was 4.5 percent of Warsaw's total area. Jews in the ghetto were overseen by their own police and for two years were forced to work intensively for the *Wermacht*. Isolated and suffering from hunger, exhaustion and disease, they were dying.

By July 1942 around 100,000 people had passed away. July 1942 was the beginning of the period of transfer to the gas chambers at Treblinka concentration camp where around 800,000 Jews were ultimately murdered. This transfer was a way to be rid of the elderly, the women and the children; only the young able to work were kept.

The Polish Council for the Aid of Jews was established by the Home Army (*AK*) in September 1942 although its activities were limited. The Jewish Combat Organization and Jewish Military Association also conspired against this oppression, uniting several thousand people. On 19th April 1943 SS troops under the command of Jürgen Stroop entered the ghetto to exterminate the remainder of the living Jews. They were welcomed by intense fire from houses and barricades and forced to retreat to obtain tanks and combat vehicles. The Jews fought on for three weeks, about 7,000 being killed and almost the same number being burned alive in houses. The remaining 56,000 were transfered to Treblinka. The whole Northern Quarter was burned and razed and even today, during roadworks, old bombs, missiles and human bones are discovered.

Walk: The Passion Road and the Fight of the Jews

Holocaust and heroic combat of Warsaw Jews is commemorated by the Passion Road and the Fight of the Jews unveiled in 1988. The trails was coursed in the area where the bloodiest combats were fought, the granite stones with names of fighters and victims carved in Polish and Yiddish were placed along the road.

1 Pawiak Prison

The prison built by the Russians in the 1830s was named after the adjacent Pawia Street. In the times of tsar, political opponents were imprisoned there, however, its most sinister fame was gained during World War Two when the Nazis imprisoned about 100,000 prisoners, soldiers and activists of secret organisations, as well as scientists, writers, actors and sportsmen. Also prisoners of

Pawiak were Warsaw's Mayor, S Stażyński, and the conspiracy soldier Jan Bytnar, nicknamed 'Rudy'. Rudy was rescued by his comrades during the famous action of 26th March 1943. From Pawiak prisoners were taken to German concentration camps and for executions in Palmiry. Later, Polish citizens were shot in the ruins of the Ghetto. Prior to the Warsaw Uprising, on July 30th 1944, the prison was partially evacuated. The remaining prisoners were shot during the uprising. On August 21st Pawiak was blown up and today the area left by the prison passes through Jana Pawła II Street, a granite plaque indicating the place where the women's prison once stood. From Dzielna Street you can see the surviving part of prison's ground floor and a dead tree which once stood in a

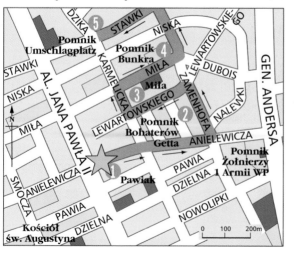

courtyard. This area is now the courtyard of the Prison Museum which has a monument to the victims of Pawiak. The museum offers a partially original, partially reconstructed exhibition of the prison history and also authentic cells with original furnishings.

2 Monument to Ghetto Heroes

The monument to Ghetto Heroes (*Pomnik Bohaterów Getta*) is located by the square of the same name, which you'll find between Anielewicza Zamenhofa and Karmelicka, Lewartowskiego. It was unveiled shortly after World War Two, in 1948, and commemorates the heros of the Ghetto in the form of a huge block built of basalt rock with a group of figures emerging from its centre. The monument presents the rebels fighting for their inevitable death to be an honourable one. In 1970, German Chancellor Willi Brandt knelt in front of the monument. It is within this

The bridge joining two parts of the Ghetto

square that the construction of the Jews of Poland Historical Institute is planned.

3 Miła Street / Monument to Bunker

On the junction of Miła Street and Dubois Street is a monument, in the form of a mound with a headstone, to the leader of Ghetto Uprising M Anielewicz, who lost his life.

4/5 Umschlagplatz Square and Monument

This walking tour finishes at Umschlagplatz Square, in the place where a railway siding was located and where Jews were loaded into goods wagons. The trains transferred around 300,000 people to Oświęcim (*Auschwitz*) and Treblinka. The monument here is sometimes called the Monument to the Three Hundred Thousand (*Pomnik Trzystu Tysięcy*). A simple monument comprising a white marble wall covered with names, it symbolises the Wailing Wall and that wall which once surrounded the Ghetto, separating Jews from the regular life of the city.

Dead tree at Pawiak Prison

Cemeteries

Warsaw is a city proud of its historical cemeteries, which have provided a final resting place for people of various religious persuasions and which survived the war while the rest of the city was razed. It is recommended to visit not only the well-known cemeteries but also the lesser-known necropolis located at the Warsaw limits, swathed in greenery and containing extraordinary graves of various religious persuasions.

Simple Graves of the Home Army Soldiers

The largest number of cemeteries is to be found within the Powązki quarter, providing a place of eternal rest for generations of politicians, scholars, writers and artists. From 1790 to 1918, cemeteries were considered an important factor in the shaping and preservation of national identity. The funerals of famous Poles were changing into patriotic manifestations, the best example of which was the funeral of the national composer Moniuszko in 1872 and the writer Prus in 1912 in which thousands of Poles participated.

In the catacombs located close to St Charles Boromeo Church (Kościół św. Karola Boromeusza) other renowned Poles are buried, such as Staszic, the co-

Powązki Cemetery

author of the Constitution of the 3rd May, poet F Bohomolec and architect Merlini who also designed some of the gravestones here. In 1925 the 'Avenue of the Meritorious' *(Aleja Zasłużonych)* was erected and the first to be buried here was noble-prized W Reymont. There are also the tombs of writer Boleslaw Prus, inscribed with *Serce serc* (The Heart of the Heart), also the poet Staff, opera singer Jan Kiepura and lately director Krzysztof Kieślowski. Also not far from the St Charles Boromeo Church is the grave of the composer S Moniuszko (whose coffin was initially placed in the catacombs) by its side is the tomb of Chopin's parents.

In the old part of the Powązki cemetery are the graves of a poet Kazimiera Iłłakowiczówna, who after the war lived in Poznań but she purchased a plot in Powązki cemetery to ensure that she would make her return to Warsaw. You will also see a figure of a dog on the grave of writer and animal protector Dygasiński. There is also the military cemetery to visit, where the Cross of Katyń stands over the symbolic grave of the 4000 officers of the Polish Army.

The biggest Polish necropolis is the Roman Catholic Bródnowski Cemetery. In the interwar period Warsaw's Archbishop Kakowski and R Dmowski, a leader of the National Democratic party, were buried here. Besides the Roman Catholic cemetery Warsaw also has a Jewish cemetery (Okopowa Street), which survived the Second World War. The representatives of the Jewish community found here include Dr Zamenhof, the creator of the artificial *Esperanto* language, bookseller and publisher Samuel Orgelbrand. The statue guarding the grave

of physician, writer and thinker, Janusz Korczak shows a teacher and a writer accompanying a group of children to Hitler's concentration camp. The war almost completely damaged the Tatar Cemetery *(Cmentarz Tatarski)* where only a few graves survived.

The Evangelical-Lutheran cemetery (entrance from Młynarska Street) was designed by A Zug who was later to be buried here, in 1907. There are graves to famous chocolate producers, the Wedel family, and also the painter W Gerson. At the neighbouring Evangelical Reformed cemetery (entrance from Żytnia Street) are the graves of the writer S Żeromski and singer A German.

Another complex of cemeteries include the Jewish cemetery in the Bródno quarter, Karaim Cementary *(Cmentarz Karaimski)* in Wola and the Orthodox-Christian Cemetery *(Cmentarz Prawosławny)* also in the Wola quarter.

All Saints Day - 1st November
'Hurry to love people, they are passing away so quickly'
                              Priest Jan Twardowski

On 1st November people in Poland visit graves, taking candles and flowers as they pray in silence with their families at the graveside. Honourable guards stand nearby the graves of meritorious countrymen and soldiers. At historical cemeteries (for example Powązki and Bródno) donations are collected for the restoration of graves and tombs, some of which are considered to be works of art. In the evening the glow of candlelight reminds the people of Poland of those people and moments in history which may well be passed but must always be remembered.

Tours

Warsaw's surroundings are packed with interesting places and historical sites which make excellent one-day tours. Just a few kilometres from Warsaw you'll find, for example, the Romanesque basilica in Czerwińsk, Royal Pułtusk and recreational areas such as Zegrzyński Impoundment Lake.

Pine trees in Łuża

Kampinoska Woodlands

You'll find Kampinoska woodlands about 40km from the city centre. The journey there is via Kampinos and Leszno.

Also worthy of attention, besides the woodlands themselves, are the manor houses found in Kampinos, Granica and Tułowice Kampinos, once a base for Polish kings such as John III Sobieski or

The chapel in the Collegiate in Pułtusk

Stanislaus Augustus Poniatowski when they went hunting in the forests. In the village is a timber 18th-century church with two towers and a 19th-century brick manor. It was here within the classical manor house that the rebel leader of the January Uprising had his headquarters. The beautiful views of woodlands stretch out and away from the terrace.

In Granica village an early 20th-century manor house is located, seat of the Kampinoski National Park Museum with its rich collections of fauna and flora samples. Kampinoska Woodlands is also a habitat for boars, deer, beavers, moose, cranes, corncrakes and black storks, and the museum organises guided tours into the woodlands to watch animal life, go birdwatching and enjoy campfire talks. Not far away from the museum is the Ethnographic Outdoor Museum, set in a thatch-roofed house.

In Tułowice, in the 1980s, the painter A Nowak-Zempliński set about rebuilding an old manor. Originally built at the end of the 18th century it retains an old carriage shed with a collection of old carriages, all typical of Mazovia and Małopolska regions.

Pułtusk

Pułtusk is located about 60km from
Warsaw and is best approached from
Legionowo. A trip to Pułtusk offers you
another chance to enjoy the great
outdoors and be amongst nature. Pułtusk
lies close to the Narew River within the
Narwiański National Park, and the river
forks into two arms surrounding Pułtusk
old town. Boulevards, bridges, canoes and
yachts give Pułtusk a Venetianesque
character, parts of preserved defensive
walls adding medieval
character. By canoeing
or yachting along the
arms of the Narew you
can reach the Augustów
lakes. Also accessible
and worthy of attention
are the edges of Biała
Woodlands *(Puszcza
Biała)*, areas particularly
recommended for
biking, horse riding or
walking. The woodland
is an epicentre of Kurpie
region's cultural
heritage. 1000-year-old
Pułtusk, with its 16th-
century Renaissance
castle, became a
meeting place for Polish
ex-pats and was called
Polonia. In 1989, the
House of Polonia was
opened in the castle.
The castle is now open
for visitors and its
restored halls house an
art gallery, a concert hall
and can be used for
conferences. Folk music

is played for guests and the hotel (*Dom
Polonia*) restaurants tempt you with
traditional Polish cuisine; our tip is crayfish
soup *(zupa rakowa)* or game roast
(pieczeń z dziczyzny). While in the
vicinity why not pick up some typical
Pułtusk produce, perhaps red glazed
pottery, Kurpie pattern carpers or honey
from Biała Woodlands.

All roads in Pułtusk lead visitors to the
400m x 40m Market Square *(Rynek)*, one
of the longest in Europe, which in the

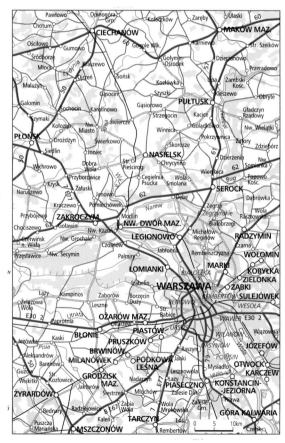

Boats by Zegrzyński Impoundment Lake

19th century was divided into separate stripe-shaped places of trade. Today the market is surrounded by townhouses yet in the very centre is a town hall with a clock tower, a seat to the municipal authorities and historical museum.

The name of the town Pułtusk was carved on the Arc de Triomphe in Paris by order of Napoleon who was satisfied with his military campaign of 1806, near Pułtusk. Pułtusk's churches form the background of the novel *The memories of the Navy Blue Uniform* by W Gomulicki who describes his youth and schooldays in Pułtusk. The author's school was situated at the Jesuit monastery. In 1990 the Renaissance polychrome painting was discovered in the Collegiate Church. During renovation, under the layer of white paint, a multicoloured painting appeared.

Zegrzyński Impoundment Lake

Zegrzyński Impoundment Lake is located about 40km from Warsaw and is reached via Jabłonna village. The lake was created in 1963 when waters of Narew River were dammed, creating an area of 33km² with a maximal depth of 15m. Now a watersports centre, it has the biggest number of recreational facilities on the eastern side. The lake joins the Vistula River via the Żerański Channel *(Kanał Żerański)* and this is the route used by sailors and canoers to reach the huge lakes of the Mazury region. The main town in the area is Serock, also located by Narew River. An historical burgh, dated about 11-13th century was discovered at the edge of the present town and you will also find a late-Gothic church, founded in the 16th century by Mazovia Dukes.

Czersk

Czersk is located about 39km from Warsaw and is reached via the towns of Piaseczno and Góra Kalwaria, the distance between the main road and the Market Hall in Czersk being about 1km. It is hard to believe, but Czersk was the main administrative centre of Mazovia in the 13th century when Duke Konrad I built his burgh here. In the 14th century the Czersk Dutchy and its church hierarchy supervised the developing Warsaw and Warsaw depended upon Czersk. This medieval excellence is remembered every year during the European Heritage Days. Perhaps the most interesting event is organized in spring, the so-called Queen Bona Gardens *(Ogrody Królowej Bony),* which commemorates the Queen Bona Sforza who founded gardens, vineyards and orchards in this area. The Italian-born Queen visited Czersk on various occasions and always enjoyed her stay.

Czersk lost its municipal rights in 1969 and is no longer a town, it does however remain a famous orcharding centre. Orchards are located high on the scarps by Vistula. Try to visit Czersk when the apple blossom is in full bloom.

There is also a small ruined Gothic castle to discover and a small market square set about 1km from busy roads. The castle is attractive with a preserved tower gate, two keeps and fairly lengthy parts of original defensive walls. The bridge over the moat was built in the 18th century by Marshal Bieliński who wanted to protect this deserted castle which is now regarded as a romantic ruin.

Czerwińsk

Once upon a time Czerwińsk was accessible only via Vistula River, now it can be easily reached via a good road from Jabłonna village to Nowy Dwór Mazowiecki and Zakroczym.

The small village of Czerwińsk is located in the high scarp and is famous for one of Mazovia's most precious historical sites, the Romanesque Basilica of the Holy Virgin Mary *(Bazylika Najświętszej Marii Panny)* built in 1155. The reddish stone used for the basilica's construction gave this town its name (red = czerwony = Czerwińsk). Czerwińsk also has its very own place in Polish history. Here in July 1410 the united armies under the command of the Polish king Ladislas Jagiełło *(Władysław Jagiełło)* were praying for victory before the famous battle of Grunwald. Knights sharpened their swords on the church's portal, the cavities and

smashes are still visible today in the bottom part of the portal. These knights believed that the power of the place would pass on into their swords as they went onwards to fight, successfully, against the Teutonic Order on the fields of Grunwald. A victorious Polish king returned to the church at Czerwińsk and left a part of his armour as an offering. The bronze plaque in the south wall of the church commemorated 1410 Grunwald Battle victory. Between 1903-12 the basilica was renovated and now is in quite good condition. It has three naves with two towers and baroque furnishings. Romanesque influences can be seen in the portal and columns. The Crucifixion Chapel *(Kaplica Ukrzyżowania)* holds very precious fresco paintings (about 10m² in area) in which medieval artists present the history of world creation, Noah and the Ark, Original Sin and Abraham's alliance with God. Other valuable elements are the *Pieta* and ornaments residing in the presbytery, and a painting above the high altar of the Holy Mother of Consolation *(Matka Boska Pocieszenia)*, dated 1612, is regarded as miraculous.

A monastery was built here in 1328 and the ex-refectory is now a chapel. The monastery also hosts a museum.

Not less interesting is the bell tower dated 1497 with a huge bell weighing 1360kg called Prince Royal Kazimierz.

Romanesque portal of the basilica in Czerwińsk

Żelazowa Wola

Żelazowa Wola, a real mecca for those who love the music of Frederic Chopin, is located about 52km from Warsaw and is accessible via Kampinos village.

It is here that you will find Chopin's parents' house, which was in fact the outbuilding of the Count Skarbek's family where Chopin's father was employed as a French teacher. Chopin's father, Nicholas a Frenchman, married the Polish girl Tekla Justyna Krzyżanowska and according to the local church birth records Frederic was born on 22nd February 1810. The manor is currently changing hands and is not open to the public. In 1928 the Friends of Frederic Chopin's House Society created a museum. Many souvenirs were lost during the Second World War but the atmosphere of the house is recalled by period furnishings and family portraits of Chopin and his family, photographs taken by Bisson, one of Paris's first photographers.

From spring to autumn, in the courtyard of the Chopin's, music concerts are organised. Artists arrive from Poland and abroad while the audience sits on benches or walks in the park. In the park are a few monuments to Frederic, for example, an obelisk with the F Chopin medallion dated 1894. In winter, concerts are organised inside the manor house of the Frederic Chopin Society.

Radziejowice

Radziejowice town is located about 42km from Warsaw and is accessible via Katowice Route *(Szosa Katowicka)*.

Radziejowice is known for its beautiful park, palace and scenic surroundings. Unfortunately the Radziejowski family is regarded as rather infamous. During the 17th-century Polish-Swedish Wars, Warsaw surrendered to the Swedish army. Hieronim Radziejowski, the state clerk, openly supported the Swedish king. The next Radziejowski of note, Michał, was the primate during Swedish occupation of Warsaw in 1704. Radziejowski changed the Polish kings according to the Swedish king's orders, exchanging and dethroning August II Wettin and crowning Stanislaus Leszczyński. This exchange was only temporary and soon this primate had to

The manor and park in Żelazowa Wola

Palace and park in Radziejowice

flee from Poland. Michał Radziejowski reconstructed and remodelled the palace into its baroque form. Those coming after him, however, did not take proper care of the palace. The next owner the Karsiński family (1782-1945) ordered its reconstruction into a romantic neo-Gothic castle using elements from the old baroque building.

There is a plaque embedded into a wall which commemorates the visit of King Sigismond III Vasa in 1606. Polish kings visited Radziejowice very willingly because of its short distance to Jaktorowska Woodlands *(Puszcza Jaktorowska)* where they often went hunting. Now the palace belongs to the Ministry of Culture and Art and visitors can come here for a walk or

for a meal at the palace restaurant.

Jabłonna

Jabłonna is located about 20km from the city centre and is accessible via Żerań quarter *(Modlińska Street)*.

The palace in Jabłonna deserves inclusion on every itinerary. Once owned by Prince Józef Poniatowski, heroic commander during the Napoleonic wars and favourite of woman, its many features include an orangery, Poniatowski's Arch *(Łuk Poniatowskiego)*, the ruins of a grotto, and a horse and carriage shed that is open to the public. The palace, built in 1646, remodelled by Marconi between 1827 and 1851 into classical form and burnt down by the Germans during World War Two, was

Classical church in Opiniogóra

reconstructed and furnished with furniture from the classicism period. The left wing of the palace *(Royal)* is a seat of the Diplomatic Club, the right is used as a Conference Centre for the Polish Academy of Science (PAN).

Twierdza Modlin (Modlin Fortress)

Modlin is about 35km from Warsaw is accessible from Legionowo and or by train from the Gdański Railway Station *(Dworzec Gdański).*

On the arms of the rivers entwining Warsaw few strongly guarded fortresses defending the city were built. One of them, the Modlin, was a fortress established by Napoleon in the years 1807-12. In Napoleon's times Modlin fortress was built in a half-oval shape with five bastions, open from the river's side and with a square redoute enclosed by water.

Scientists claim that this two-floored fortress was designed by Napoleon and is the only one authored by the French caesar. From the upper floor more distant targets could be shot at while the bottom floor protected the access to the moat. The Modlin Fortress offered shelter for rebels of the November Uprising and, in the 19th century the Russians rebuilt the Modlin Fortress enabling it to become the most powerful Russian fortress in the area of the Polish Kingdom. It consisted of three rings with 50km-long circuit of outer ring was creating modern concrete fort.

Opinogóra

Opinogóra is located 115km from Warsaw and it is accessible from the town of Ciechanów.

Opiniogóra possesses a little castle with a high turret. In 1843 Wincenty Krasiński a father of the famous poet Zygmunt Krasiński bought the castle and gave it to his son as a wedding present. Zygmunt had three children whose names were also given to neighbouring villages Władysławowo, Zygmuntowo and Elżbiecin.

Poniatowski's Arch at the park in Jabłonna

Today there is a Museum of Romanticism *(Muzeum Romantyzmu)* portraying the third poet of Polish Romanticism after A Mickiewicz and J Słowacki. Interestingly there are portraits of Zygmunt Krasiński as a five-year-old boy in the uniform of a chevau-leger soldier *(szwoleżer)*, who together with the young Chopin were stated as

The former casino in Modlin

wonderful children of Warsaw. A souvenir from the Napoleonic period comes in the form of one of Napoleon's briefcases. It was bought from private owners in the Ukraine and has since been exhibited in Moscow, St Petersburg and Kiev as well as back in the Ukraine.

Konstancin-Jeziorna

Konstancin is about 20km from the city centre and is also accessible by bus. Konstancin is touching the Botanical Garden in Powsin and it is about 5km from the administrative limits of Warsaw.

Konstancin has the status of 'health resort' and the very name Konstancin was taken after the first name of Count Skórzewski's mother who took a decision to change this little village into such: a luxurious health resort. The leading spa is the Motor System Revalidation Centre (STOCER) known for its achievements in Poland and abroad. In the Spa Park *(Park Uzdrowiskowy)* is a thermal brine spring *(źródło solankowe)*, graduation towers *(tężnie)*, and so-called *inhalatorium*. Konstancin itself bathes in greenery with its old villas set between the trees. The

villas were built by illustrious architects in various styles, newer ones built sympathetically in relation to the older ones. Neighbouring Jeziorna is situated by the Jeziorka River and was probably found in the 15th century. The area of Jeziorka River has interesting connotations. Despite duels in the 19th century in Warsaw were forbidden but outside Warsaw borders they were provided. The most famous duel was between adventurer Casanova and a Polish magnate of doubtful reputation F K Branicki.

Villa *Netemi* in Kontacin

Varsovian Folklore

Bard of Warsaw, Stanisław Grzesiuk, sang a song about 'crafty' people living in Warsaw. Grzesiuk was born in the Czerniaków quarter and despite the fact that the narrow streets of his day have become wide roads and the old tenements were replaced by new blocks of flats, some people do still live in the world of Grzesiuk's songs. These ballads of the 'crafty' people i.e. local underground, so-called *lumpenproletariat* or those people colliding with the law who were tough, good and honourable somehow maintained their relevance through the war years and beyond.

Another bard of Warsaw was Stefan Wiechecki. His colourful characters

lived in the Praga quarter and had typical features and methods of speaking, and his heroes were tough, humble, witty and strong. They spoke using characteristic slang and they also used softer consonants with 'y' often appearing instead of 'i'. Besides slang, Warsaw folklore has strong roots in Warsaw's taverns where a typical meal is vodka and obligatory appetizers of herrings and so called special jelly called *Nóżki* (pig legs brew, vegetables put into a bowl and chilled in the fridge become a jelly!). Another must within Warsaw folklore is a typical dinner by the name of *Varsovian Tribes (Flaczki po warszawsku*; cut intestines with vegetables and spices, boiled in spicy broth) or potato spherical dumplings stuffed with meat called *Pyzy z mięsem*.

When Warsaw was being reconstructed on the left side of the river, with its palaces mostly restored and the right side remaining more or less original and only slightly touched, the right had its own atmosphere with close relationships between families and neighbours. To delve into some of this folklore take a visit to Brzeska, Ząbkowska, Kijowska where some of the old sign boards and stucco works remain and there are secret passages known only to the locals. The main trade centre in Praga quarter is Targowa Street where goods are sold directly from hand to hand, from

tables and pavements. Nothing, however, compares to Różycki's Bazaar *(Bazar Różyckiego)* spreading between

Targowa, Ząbkowska, Brzeska, and Kępna, and founded in 1901 by a rich pharmacist called Julian Różycki. An area related with trade for around 350 years, here you can buy more or less everything. Różycki's Bazaar is a main strand within the folklore which lives on in the Praga quarter, as are the songs sung by the Chmielna Street Orchestra or a newer Szwagierkolaska band. Catch the Chmielna Street Orchestra in Chmielna Street or in Dmowski Rondo in the heart of Warsaw (see *Cultural Praga p144-5*).

Far Left: One of the unpaved streets in Warsaw - Ząbkowska in the Praga quarter
Left: Bazar Różyckiego
Above: The entrance to Różycki's Bazaar

Getting Away

Warsaw's urbanisation has taken place with surprising ease, to the extent that the city's elderly remember the more distant districts as virgin and difficult to reach while it is these same districts that have suddenly become integral parts of the capital.

A metal sculpture in a park near Królikarnia

The Zoo

Despite their not being united within a single municipal organism, the right bank of Warsaw has always shared the history of the left, and with the Praga quarter incorporated into Warsaw back in 1791. Here on land close to the Vistula near the end of Śląsko-Dąbrowski Bridge *(Most Śląsko-Dąbrowski)*, the huge Praski Park was founded in 1871, where from 1900 the *Lunapark* and *Praski Theatre* stood. Today the area is a park with dozens of old avenues. In 1927 some parts were separated in order to found the zoo which was, by the standards of the time, modern and built with great drive. The zoo is the right bank's main attraction, a place where families come to see exotic animals while in the Fairy Garden, they could pay a visit to the perhaps more

An Indian rhinoceros at Warsaw Zoo

familiar donkeys, ponies and guinea pigs.

Cerkiew Prawosławna (The Orthodox Church)

The byzantine Orthodox Church, on Targowa Street, with its gold-plated domes is certainly an exotic sight. More correctly known as The Mary Magdalene Metropolitan Orthodox Church, it was consecrated on 29th June 1869 and managed to survive the Second World War with its original furnishings intact.

Lasek Bielański (Bielański Woods)

In the 18th, 19th and 20th centuries a strong Varsovian custom at Whitsun, along with attendance of Holy Mass was a trip to the Bielański Woods. Indeed the Kings August II Wettin and August III Wettin travelled to Bielański Woods quite frequently yet the area was also popular with commoners who made their way there by all possible means of transport. Carousels and devil mills turned and the visitors danced in wooden *tanzbuden*. The nearby quarter of Młociny also offered great entertainment and the place known as *Parkowa Góra,* previously the destination of longer expeditions, is now considered to be located within Warsaw's boundaries. The Bielański Woods also include a nature reserve with an educational trail of boards and a map, this abutting the building of the Academy of Physical Education. Close to another Academy, that of Catholic Theology, is the Church of the Immaculate Conception *(KościółNiepokalanego Poczęcia)* which has the coat of arms of Poland, Lithuania and Camaldolese Order mounted on the front wall. The complex was demolished during the Second World War and the Camaldolese monks have returned only recently.

Królikarnia Palace

Warsaw also grew in a southerly direction where deep in the park on Puławska Street in the Mokotów quarter is a palace called Królikarnia, which at the time of the Wettin dynasty housed a rabbit *(królik)* breeding farm. Later, the park was bought by Count Thomatis, a theatre director during the reign of Stanislaus Augustus Poniatowski, who built the palace there. Many owners followed including Marta Krasińska who before the Second World War managed a hospice for the terminally ill.

Today the palace hosts an exhibition gifted to the nation by the artist and sculptor Xavery Dunikowski, which presents the work of artists who once stayed at the concentration camp in Oświęcim, or Auschwitz. During post-war remodelling the palace received its classical Roman form with ornaments and a stone portico housing allegories of art and science in the arched entranceways.

Pałacyk Szustra (Szuster's Palace)

At the heart of the Mokotów quarter, on the scarp sloping down to the Vistula, is

Orthodox Christian Church, Praga quarter

Szuster's Palace which was founded by Duchess Elżbieta Czartoryska-Lubomirska in the 18th century, with a new park, modelled on the French Château de Versailles. All of the buildings of the complex, together with a fishing village and ponds, the towers by the entrance and a small maisonette in Mauritanian style, were designed by S B Zug. In 1845 this corner of Mokotów was taken over by the Warsaw lithographer Franciszek Szuster, and now the palace belongs to the Warsaw Music Society who, on Sundays and Thursdays, organise classical music concerts.

Zespół pałacowo-parkowy w Wilanowie (The Palace and Park in Wilanów)

The Wilanów complex stands at the end of the Royal Tract and recalls a glorious period of Polish history, the 1683 Victory at Vienna, a battle won under the command of the Polish king, John III Sobieski. This palace was the seat of a king who appreciated family life and military success in equal measure.

The Palace

The palace was built for the royal couple John III Sobieski and his queen, Marie Casimire d'Arquien Sobieska at the end of the 17th century and was inherited by the king's sons in 1696. In 1720 it was taken over by several Polish magnates, yet retained the status of royal residence to become in 1730 seat of the king once more, this time of August II Wettin and then August III Wettin. In 1805 the archeologist and art collector Stanisław Kostka Potocki founded here one of the first museums to be opened to the public. Wilanów was to be remodelled several times, always by remarkable architects.

The ground floor of the main building is furnished with original items from the time of John III Sobieski and Marie Casimire d'Arquien Sobieska. In the queen's bedroom the walls are covered with baroque fabric while in the king's there is a bed with a baldachin canopy made of Turkish fabrics won at Vienna. The palace is also home to the

Portrait Gallery *(Galeria Portretu)* where coffin portraits are exhibited, and to the Etruscan Room *(Gabinet Etruski)* with its surviving collection of antiques. In the south wing, the bathroom and apartments of Duchess Izabella Lubomirska survived while in the Grand Vestibule *(Wielka Sień)* are decorations by Zug including classical furnishings and baroque allegories of the four elements.

Grobowiec Potockich (Potocki Tomb)

This neo-Gothic tomb was built by A Potocki for his parents Stanisław Kostka Potocki and Aleksandra Potocka in the years 1834-36. It was designed by E Marconi and is decorated with the figures of lions and the coats of arms of two families, the Potocki and the Lubomirski.

Orangery

The 18th-century Orangery harbours an exhibition called the *Polish Arts and Crafts from the Wilanów Historical Collection* which is comprised of 430 items gathered by Wilanów's owners. The items on display come from excellent workshops and they include Poland's largest collection of biscuit pottery which is fired but unglazed porcelain or, rarely, faience pottery, as well as objects made of china and gold, and clocks and products of Far Eastern origin.

Park

Founded in the 17th century in old French style, this geometric park of hedges and trees spans two levels, its oldest part enclosing the palace. However, further on this French style merges into the English style with a section of Rose Garden *(Ogród Różany)* which was designed by S B Zug, enclosing the complex on the south side. The entire grounds occupy an area of 43 hectare and prove a wonderful setting for Wilanów Palace. Among the trees several buildings have been erected; one a neo-Gothic castle which is in fact a pumping station, also a Chinese arbour, and figures of antique gods and goddesses and decorative vases in abundance. Beyond the monument, commemorating victory at the Battle of Raszyn in 1809 which was fought between Napoleon's army and the Russians, is a man-made island that is reached by way of a Roman bridge.

Kościół św.Anny (St Anna's Church)

Surrounded by a fence depicting the stations of the Calvary Passion Road, this cross-shaped church was built in the years 1772-75 as a typical basilica in the neo-Renaissance style, but with a baroque facade. In the presbytery the original floor is preserved, made of Egyptian granite from a column in the Caesar Hadrian Temple of Peace in Rome. This was the gift of Pope Pius IX to the Duchess Aleksandra Potocka. Other surviving features are the 18th-century font and 19th-century wooden organ, along with sculptures, frescoes and paintings. Close by is a historical inn and forge adapted to serve as a restaurant called *Kuźnia,* and café *Hetmańska.*

Pałac w Natolinie (The Palace in Natolin)

The Palace in Natolin was built in 1780-82 in line with S B Zug's design and is the one of the most beautiful classical residences in the suburbs. Attractively located in a park, it is distinguished by an oval hall which opens onto a terrace and Ionian colonnade. The paintings are the work of V Brenna. Since 1799 the palace was the property of Aleksandra Lubomirska, wife of Stanisław Kostka Potocki. Potocki remodelled the palace between 1806 and 1808 according to the plans of C P Aigner and also changed the name of the village to Natolin, a move inspired by the

The park near the Orangery

couple's newborn daughter Natalia. The residence was crowned with a dome and received a new facade facing the drive plus interesting sculptural decoration on the ground floor, this produced in the famous stucco workshop of W Bauman.

In the surrounding park are several interesting structures, such as the Doric Temple, Mauritanian bridge, gate and an aqueduct constructed in 1834-38 by Marconi.

On Nowoursynowska Street close to the park is the oldest tree in Warsaw, a 1000-year-old oak named *Mieszko,* a relic of the former Mazovian Woodlands.
Address: Nowoursynowska 84

Rozkosz Palace in Ursynów Quarter

In the Ursynów district, on the scarp sloping down to the Vistula river, is another complex comprising a park and palace, this one called Rozkosz. It was established by Izabela Lubomisrka in 1775-80, although its contemporary look was provided by Z Rospendowski in 1858-60 for the new owner, L Krasiński.

At that time the facades were decorated with busts of the Polish Commanders S Czarniecki, W Koniecpolski, P Sanguszko and Jan Tarnowski, as well as those of famous women such as the legendary Wanda, the Duchess Dąbrówka and the Queens Jadwiga and Barbara. Between 1822 and 1831 the palace was owned by the writer, publicist and politician Julian Ursyn Niemcewicz and today it is occupied by the Warsaw Agricultural University (SGGW).
Address: Nowoursynowska 166

Ogród Botaniczny w Powsinie (Botanical Garden in Powsin)

Located on the Vistula scarp in 1974, this is a scientific testing station and educational centre of the Polish Academy of Science. The Botanical Garden has been open to the public since 1990 and houses a collection of 7000 species across an area of 16 hectares, protecting 150 endangered species and plants under conservation law. In the arboretum there are around 1300 species of tree, shrub

Rozkosz Palace

Królikarnia Palace in the Mokotów quarter, site of interesting exhibitions, concerts and conferences

and Ericaceous and Magnoliaceae plant, with over 3000 species of cultivated and decorative plant, roses, perennials and 200 old apple trees raised in Poland before 1939. The country's largest Iridaceae plant collection, 450 species, may be found here too, along with the largest collection of exotic species numbering around 1500.

From the beginning of May to mid-September the Botanical garden organises events including painting and photo exhibitions in the Fangora Palace, and concerts on Sundays as part of the *Floralia International Piano Festival* (Flowers in Music). The Garden is situated in Powsin which also offers other recreational facilities such as swimming pools, a paddling pool, playgrounds and tennis courts.
Address: Prawdziwka 2

Kabacki Forest

Kabacki Forest neighbours the Botanical Garden in Powsin and stretches over

almost 920 hectares, a popular walking area for Varsovians, it consists of trees with both needles and leaves, predominantly pine and oak. The history of Kabacki Forest goes back to the time of King John III Sobieski who built the pheasant farm in the village of Kabaty. At the end of the 1930s the Mayor of Warsaw, S Stażyński, bought the forest from its private owners to create a recreational area for the city's inhabitants in the south-eastern part. The last stop on the underground system is located close by.

The Botanical Garden in Powsin

Walk: Saska Kępa

Saska Kępa is located on the right bank of the Vistula and is separated from North Praga by Paderewski/Skaryszewki Park and Kamionkowskie Lake. It is one of the most scenic parts of Warsaw, the site of trips and fun days out in the 19th century. After Poniatowksi Bridge was built, Saska Kępa changed in character, and in the 1920s and 30s a new district of blocks of flats was built. *Allow 2 hours.*

Skaryszewski Park

1 Most Poniatowskiego (Poniatowski Bridge)

Józef Poniatowski Bridge and viaduct were constructed in 1904-13 and subsequently damaged twice during the Great War and the Second World War. Reconstruction was performed in 1946 by S Hempel, and widening in 1965-66. The

Holy Mother of God the Constant Aid Church

bridge has quite interesting decoration together with neo-Renaissance towers and pavilions erected in 1907-13, according to the designs of S Szyller.

2 Francuska Street

Francuska Street is the main artery through Saska Kępa and is lined with modernist houses elegantly spaced amongst the greenery. No. 2 was built by Korngold and Lubiński and is a wonderful example of functionalism in architecture.

3 KościółMatki Boskiej Nieustającej Pomocy (Holy Mother of God the Constant Aid Church)

The St Andrew Bobola Church, a P Lubiński design, was construction between 1938 and 1956, a delay in its construction due to the Second Word War. The church is known for its modernist mosaic interior and harmonious scheme of columns whilst inside is a plaque commemorating the soldiers of the 336th Infantry Regiment, which defended Saska Kępa in 1939.

4 Paderewski/ Skaryszewski Park

The founder of this park was F Szanior, the director of municipal parks between 1905-1922. It was planned according to the rules of secession and modernism in an area of 60 hectares. In walking the avenues and around the two ponds, visitors may admire the monument to the American Colonel Edward House, an advisor to US President Woodrow Wilson who openly supported Poland's regaining of independence after the Great War. The monument was established by the pianist J I Paderewski in 1932. Also worth seeing are the inter-war sculptures; Niewska's *Bathing One*, Jackowski's *Dancer,* Kuna's *Rhythm* and Biernacki's *Faun.*

5 Kamionkowskie Lake

Kamionkowskie Lake fills the old bed of the Vistula River and has witnessed several important historical events. It was here in 1572 that the first elected king, Henri de Valois, was chosen, while in 1656 the Polish-Swedish Battle of Warsaw took place nearby, a Polish victory which was later described by the national writer H Sienkiewicz in his trilogy *The Deluge.*

6 KościółMatki Boskiej Zwycięskiej (Holy Mother of God the Victorious Church)

This parish gained its church in the 13th century, but the present building was erected only recently in 1929-32, in the fashionable mannerist style. The graves around the church, relics of the old cemetery, are those of the rebels killed in the Olszynka Grochowska battle, which took place during the November Uprising (1830-31). During the church's construction some graves were

unfortunately damaged, those remains disturbed being re-buried in the crypt below the high altar.

7 Rogatki na Grochowskiej (Tollgates on Grochowska Street)

On opposite sides of Grochowska Street are two white maisonettes which are distinguished by their porches, elegant columns and the reliefs above their windows. These are old tollgates built in 1813-1818 in the classical style by the meritorious architect J Kubicki (1759-1833). They were built for a police officer and toll collector and were the beginning of the Brzeski Tract, which was remodelled into the motorway between 1820 and 1823.

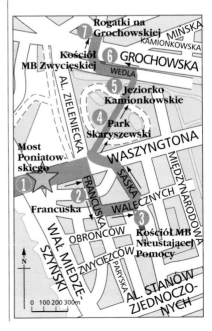

Praga began to develop in the second half of the 19th century. Industry was located here, along with three railway stations, as well as new blocks of flats that were also built. The Second World War did not affect Praga as severely as it did the left bank of the city and this is why it is possible to see what remains of the 19th-century industrial town. It is the combination of that which survived and that which was built, all factories and impressive tenements which attract the younger generation of artists looking for new horizons. Slowly the new Varsovian bohema is moving to Praga where the climate of pre-war Warsaw is preserved together with enclaves of culture.

At No.6 Inżynierska Street are the 19th-century storage rooms of a removals company where artists have established their workshops in the old outbuildings and invite visitors to view their art or advise on matters of interior design.

The *Academia* Theatre located at

No.11 Listopada Street focuses on artistic activity taking place in Praga and is famous for social initiatives which blend art with good citizenship in experiments such as *Neighbours for Neighbours*.

In the old part of Praga, at No.27-31 Ząbkowska Street, is Warsaw's oldest vodka factory, *Koneser*. Within the area of the factory the Luksfera Gallery has its home, the first commercial gallery in Warsaw to sell only photographs. They organise exhibitions and workshops for photographers, promotions of artistic posters and books on photography and host talks with artists who have chosen photography as their means of self-expression. Ząbkowska Street has been pupating as an artistic colony for a number of years. Its new appearance is easily seen from neighbouring Targowa Street, thanks to the high building with the pointed turret.

The 'artistic picnic' (when for example a group of dancers invite

ordinary people to come and dance with them in a particular place, for free) entitled *Praga is Likeable (Praga da się lubić)* links the activities of several artistic workshops, galleries, theatres *(Academia, Remus)* and music groups. This collaboration results in outdoor painting or photography sessions, street theatre, concerts or happenings. Beside Praga's own folklore, Jewish music plays a vital role here when played by *klezmer* musicians.

Ząbkowska Street is elongated by Otwocka Street where the deserted halls of an old factory here were remodelled by the composer Wojciech Trzciński over a two year period. He preserved their industrial character and exposed some of the factory machines, making them an integral part of the decoration, some even becoming furniture.

In the bar there is a sausage machine and the bar's backdrop is an illuminated wall filled with empty methylated spirits bottles, sending out the prettiest violet colour in Poland! Over an area of 3,000m², a club and performance, theatre, exhibition and conference halls have been laid out where it is possible to organise business meetings, to listen to jazz, view an exhibition or watch a show. The best artists perform here and prestigious events are held, for instance concerts of the *Warsaw Autumn* festival. A shortened version of the creator's name is now borne by the factory, *Fabryka Trzciny*. This dilapidated complex, almost 100 years old, has became one of Warsaw's most fashionable addresses, a place pulsating with culture and with the atmosphere of a students' club.

The *Nowy Praga* Theatre (*Teatr Nowy Praga*) at *Fabryka Trzciny* is not the only theatre in Praga. On the corner of Zieleniecka and Targowa *Streets is the Zygmunt Hübner Powszechny* Theatre, one of the leading theatres in the country, while in the Targówek quarter, at No. 20 Kołowa Street, is the *Rampa* Theatre, well known for its musical repertoire. The industrial atmosphere is beneficial for artists, particularly when Praga's native inhabitants are so enigmatic and challenging for them.

Left: the opening day of J Pajewski's exhibition Europe, the *Izerskie Mts. and Silk* at the Luksfera Gallery
Right: a pre-concert rehearsal at the *Fabryka Trzciny* centre

Shopping

Over the last few years Warsaw has become a huge shopping destination where visitors will find outlets ranging from the familiar stores of the world's largest firms to small antique shops. The great majority are to be found in shopping passages, small covered concourses and out-of-town shopping malls.

A stall at the biggest antiques fair at Koło

Where and what to buy

With no effort at all it is possible to buy extraordinary souvenirs in Warsaw, whether pieces of modern or folk art, albums or jewellery of interesting designs, although the local speciality is alcohol. While big-name stores are usually located in the city centre, bargains and discounted goods may be found in shops outside the city and at bazaars. As in other European cities, the best sales and promotions take place after New Year when spending power is weaker.

Sadly, Warsaw does not have a typical souvenir in the same way as Krakow for instance. While you will notice that Warsaw's Mermaid appears on many items and is an emblem on a number of gadgets, modern paintings or artistic photography of the city also make an interesting choice.

The *Stare Miasto* (Old Town) is a real mine of souvenir shops and small antiquarian booksellers. Numerous galleries and interesting shops are also located on Krakowskie Przedmieście or Nowy Świat, while a trading tradition is continued on Chmielna Street with its boutiques offering clothing, jewellery and shoes. Wiech's Passage *(Pasaż Wiecha)*, adjoining Chmielna Street and the rear of the Central Shopping Centre at No. 116-122 Marszałkowska Street, is another place with a long trading tradition and offers goods produced by well-known clothing and footwear firms.

Folk Art

Well worth visiting are the shops of the *Cepelia* chain, commercial galleries of folk art, sculpture, paintings on glass, fabrics and embroidered tablecloths, all of which make use of regional folk motifs and patterns and are recognised as being of high quality. *Cepelia* has outlets at No. 5 Konstytucji Square, No. 23-41 Krupnicza Street, No. 8 Chmielna Street, No. 7 Egipska Street and No. 59-63 Grójecka Street.

Music

Good recordings of Polish classical music are another recommendation, whether the works of Fryderyk Chopin or Krzysztof Penderecki, as is the jazz played by Polish musicians such as Adam Makowicz and

Leszek Modżer, both pianists, and the singer Urszula Dudziak - all are artists of international standard.

A wide choice of music is available at EMPIK stores, which are located at No. 15-17 Nowy Świat Street, at the Central Shopping Centre at No. 116-122 Marszałkowska Street and in the *Arcadia* gallery. On Chmielna Street is *Arka,* the old Jabłkowski Brothers' Shopping Centre, with the huge variety of books at its *Traffic* bookshop, as well as music. One of the most popular places is the bookshop *Czuły Barbarzyńca* (Tender Barbarian), where potential buyers can read on the sofas for as long as they need to be sure of their choice.

Antiques

Warsaw is not the best antiques market but amateurs are certainly able to find bargains here. The best-known antique shops are *DESA (Nowy Świat 51; Rynek Starego Miasta 4-6),* but antiques are also to be found in the galleries of the city centre or Royal Tract *(Trakt Królewski),* for example *ART DECO (Gałaczyńskiego 7), Galeria Antyków (Poznańska 23),* the *Antykwariat pod Łabędziem* gallery *(Piwna 44),* the *Polona* gallery *(Krakowskie Przedmieście 7),* the *Czarny Butik* gallery *(Nowogrodzka 25)* and *REMPEX (Krakowskie Przedmieście 4/6).*

Shopping and Entertainment Centres

Every district of Warsaw has its own shopping centre with a spacious car park, where under one roof a supermarket and small boutiques are located along with the outlets of well-known companies selling high-quality products such as cosmetics, clothing, sports equipment and footwear; for breaks in the shopping there may be coffee shops, a bowling alley or a cinema.

The *Janki* shopping centre is located about 4km beyond the city limits on Mszczonowska Street in the village of Janki. The distance travelled is compensated for by a rich choice of pursuits, as besides the shops there is a *Multiplex Cinema City* with ten air-conditioned screens, the *Power Games* arcade with driving, motorcycling and skiing simulators, video games and billiards, and *Restrauma*, a complex of 12 restaurants offering Polish, American, Greek, Italian, Lebanese and Chinese cuisines.

The *Bemowo* shopping gallery located at No. 126 Powstańców Śląskich Street also possesses a *Multiplex Cinema City*, along with a bowling alley, restaurant and bar.

The shopping gallery *Mokotów* has

The multi-storey bookshop and club, Traffic

shops, a *Multiplex Cinema City* with 14 screens, *Top Floor Entertainment* with its bowling alley, arcade machines, billiard tables and area for a game called *cymbergaj,* not to mention 16 eating establishments.

Promenade on 75 Ostrobramska Street in the South Praga quarter offers a shopping centre, but also relaxation at its 13-screen *Multiplex Cinema City* and *Entertainment Centre Las Vegas,* the latter home to a bowling alley, billiards, *cymbergaj,* a playroom and darts. There are also 11 eating establishments, including *Star City Dinner, Pizza Hut, Dunkin Donuts* and the café *Pożegnanie z Afryką.*

Best Mall Shopping Centre in the Dolny Mokotów district has a three-dimensional cinema, the *Panasonic Imax,* as well as a *Multiplex Cinema City,* the *Entertainment Centre Hokus Pokus* with bowling, an artificial climbing wall, billiard tables and computer games, and eight restaurants and cafés.

Wola Park at No. 124 Górczewska Street offers a shopping mall, a cinema and a fitness club.

The *Arkadia* shopping centre at the Radosław roundabout is probably the largest in Europe and has a vast number of shops, but beyond this only the *Multikino* cinema.

Supermarkets

On the outskirts of Warsaw are the enormous warehouse-like outlets of the international shopping chains, where everything seems to be for sale. The city also offers huge supermarkets open seven days a week, though on Sundays their closing times move to 6pm from the usual 9pm; *Auchan, Carrefour, Geant, Real* and *Tesco* are open 24 hours a day.

Pottery available at *Cepelia*

Bazaars

The bazaar tradition is a great one, which continues still. Old Warsaw had its Marywil and Pociejów and the pre-war *Hala Mirowska* and *Koszyki* which have survived communism; Różycki's Bazaar and the bazaar on Polna Street also came through socialism successfully. When in the shops the shelves were empty, the bazaars offered fresh fruit and vegetables from around the world, and by 1989 this form of trading was everywhere, even lapping up against the Palace of Science and Culture. Now there is the gigantic Europe Fair *(Jarmark Europa)* at Dziesięciolecia Stadium *(Stadion X-Lecia)* on Zieleniecka Street, the largest, where visitors may buy almost anything; the goods come from the whole of Eastern Europe, and even from Turkey, China and Vietnam. Now too, each district also has its own bazaar or market square, where flowers, fruit and vegetables are particularly worth buying. The best fruit and vegetable bazaar is still the one at No. 9-11 Polna Street, although good fruit, vegetables and food generally are on sale in *Hala Mirowskie* at No.1 Mirowski Square, as well as in *Hala Banacha* on Kopińska Street in the Ochota district. The majority of the city's bazaars are run hygienically and in accordance with trading regulations so that meat, fish or dairy products can be bought without any worry.

Those searching for old or antique items should visit the so-called *targ staroci*, the largest of which is the Koło Antiquated Items Fair on the corner of Obozowa and Ciołka Streets in the Wola quarter. This bazaar is open seven days a week, yet at weekends it is visited by a greater number

An exclusive shopping centre in the Wola quarter

of non-professional tradespeople with something to sell, and good prices for original items become more likely.

Alcohol

Many Polish beverages make good gifts. The most highly-ranked is undoubtedly a vodka called *Żubrówka,* a typically Polish dry herbal vodka with a characteristic flavour and taste. It is made of the highest-quality alcohol and the extract of a grass harvested in the Białowieska Woodlands *(Puszcza Białowskieska),* which exists only there. Another classic is *Chopin Vodka,* which is sold in special bottles.

However the most traditional Polish beverage is not one made of either grain or potatoes. It is mead, or *miód pitny,* which comes in three varieties according to the proportions of honey and water; these are *półtorak* , *dwójniak,* and *trójniak,* all characterised by a subtle aroma and taste.

Entertainment and Nightlife

Warsaw offers such a rich array of entertainment and culture that even the fussiest will find something to suit their taste. The city's theatres present a repertoire of the highest quality, while offerings from around the world are shown in cinemas. In spring many outdoor events take place and then the promenades and parks fill with tables and outdoor cafés, and Warsaw's club scene comes highly recommended too.

A modern Imax cinema on the edge of Warsaw

Practical Information

Every day something cultural is taking place in Warsaw, the only problem is choosing the right event. Good information may be found in the Friday edition of the newspaper *Gazeta Wyborcza* in the supplement *Co jest grane*, which presents both cinema and theatre listings along with reviews of films and plays; there is also clubbing information. The weekly *Wprost* also offers its fortnightly cultural supplement *WiK - Wprost i Kultura*.

In many bars, clubs and restaurants free booklets and leaflets on cultural events are to be found, such as *City Magazine* and *Aktivist,* which contain reviews and essays. Equally, in hotels the English-language booklets on cultural life in the capital *Warsaw: What, Where, When* are available, while information may of course also be found on the Internet at, for example, www.gazeta.pl, www.onet.pl and www.um.warszawa.pl. The majority of the city's theatres, cinemas and clubs also have their own websites with listings and announcements.

Buying and Selling Tickets

Tickets are sold directly by event organisers at the box office, but also at ZASP *(Aleje Jerozolimskie 25, telephone +48 22 621 94 54)* and in EMPIK stores *(Nowy Świat 15/17, telephone +48 22 625 12 19; Marszałkowska Street 106/122, telephone +48 22 551 44 37).*

Opera and Theatre

The renowned stages of the National Philharmonic *(Filharmonia Narodowa),* National Opera and Great Theatre *(Teatr Wielki)* represent the highest standards of performance, and host local ensembles and visiting guests alike. Good music is also played at the Academy of Music *(Akademia Muzyczna)* in the Okólnik district, where students play Chopin's music, and at Szuster's Palace, while classical music is played in the stylish interiors of Wilanów Palace, the Royal Castle and the relatively modern interiors of Ujazdowki Palace. In addition, regular concerts take place at the Evangelical-Reformed Church on *al. Solidarności,* the excellent acoustics even drawing the

Warsaw Chamber Opera *(Warszawska Opera Kameralna)* which is known for its *Mozart Festivals (Festiwal Mozartowski).* Several Catholic churches also organise Passion concerts *(Misteria)* and carol singing.

The *Roma* Musical Theatre stages operettas and plays with music at their heart, while musicals are also shown at the *Syrena (The Threepenny Opera), Rampa (Magician from Lublin)* and *Żydowski (Fiddler on the Roof)* theatres. Even such notable institutions as the *Dramatyczny* Theatre or *Ateneum* welcome folk, jazz and rock music stars, though the greatest events are staged at the Congress Hall *(Sala Kongresowa).*

Fringe and experimental theatres are welcome at the Cultural Centres *(Dom Cultury)* and frequently at *Stara Prochownia* at No.2 Boleść Street. The former industrial complex *Fabryka Trzciny* at No.14 Okopowa Street with its *Teatr Nowy Praga* offers art exhibitions and jazz concerts. One of the best events is *Warsaw Underground Jazz,* or *WuJek,* which presents underground, improvised jazz.

Warsaw also possesses the *Małgorzata*

Potocka Sabat Revue Theatre, which is modelled on the pre-war revue theatres *Morskie Oko* and *Qui pro quo,* and offers not only performances and music, but also good meals and good fun.

Another cultural institution is the *Kordegarda* gallery on Krakowskie Przedmieście, where visitors may see exhibitions and listen to music in the evenings. Music has even marched into the most respected of exhibition halls, *Zachęta,* which now organises the *International Festival of Contemporary Improvised Music (Międzynarodowy Festiwal Współczesnej Muzyki Improwizowanej)* as part of the 'great Zachęta aerating action'. Zachęta is tired of its classical, traditional role and now often hosts innovators in photography too, at the *Artistic Photography Festival (Festival Fotografii Artystycznej).*

Finally, the Modern Art Centre at Ujazdowski Palace does not lack an ear for music and is famed for experimental installations and happenings – this is the place to see all that is considered vanguard.

A performance at the *Sabat* Revue Theatre

Cinemas

In 1989, after the political changes in Poland, a new type of cinema called a 'multiplex' began to be built in Warsaw. These huge buildings with their dozens of screens and rich repertoire are present at almost every shopping centre, attracting thousands wishing to combine shopping with film-going.

The more demanding film-goer however may prefer to visit those cinemas which have withstood commercial

The entrance to the *Muranów* cinema

activity and continue to lure film fans with their small rooms and ambitious screenings. One such is the 50-year-old *Muranów* Cinema *(Kino Muranów)*, which uses the slogan from Lenin's work, *'The most important art for us is film'*. Others include the *Zbyszek* and *Gerard,* which after their last rebuild are probably the cosiest in Warsaw. *Muranów* is home to a small shop with books and recordings and the *Café Kino,* where a film may be discussed after viewing. The *Luna* on Marszałkowska Street near Zbawiciela Square has a diverse repertoire and two freshly-refurnished halls; it particularly attracts the romantics and lovebirds amongst us, for whom double chairs are provided.

The National Film Stock Library *(Folmoteka Narodowa)* owns the cinema *Iluzjion* and has also been active for 50 years, although it has often relocated. It has finally found a home in the old *Stoloica* cinema at No. 50a Nartutta Street in the Mokotów quarter and attracts film-

goers with its old, truly communist-era quality and repertoire. It is especially well-known for its *Film Marathons (Maraton Filmowy)* featuring a variety of films, from classical Hollywood tear-jerkers to European, Polish and Latin American. A film session is accompanied by live music played on piano or organ. Furthermore, the *Iluzjon* cinema has access to all of the films gathered by the National Film Stock Library.

Clubs

There are many venues in Warsaw which offer good music played in comfortable interiors. One of the most interesting is *Tygmont* at No. 6-8 Mazowiecka Street where Polish jazz stars such as Zbigniew Namysłowski and Jarosław Śmietana give concerts, although clubbers too may dance to their swinging tunes. The publisher of the most respected Polish jazz magazine, *Jazz Forum,* organises its festivals here.

The *Jadłodajnia Filozoficzna* at No. 33

Dobra Street is a candidate for recognition as an artistic club, being a place where not only concerts are held, but also openings and dance events; NuJazz, reggae, ethno and punk rock are played here. A more typical venue is *Metro Jazz Club* at No. 99a Marszałkowska Street, home to the famous Jan Ptaszyn Wróblewski Quartet.

Beyond these, the *Hybrydy* club at No. 7-9 Złota Street in the heart of the capital is well worth visiting, a place known to several generations of Varsovians which has existed here for 50 years. The club opened in 1957 and hosted interesting events and the concerts of many jazz celebrities from Poland and abroad. The multi-storey building now contains the restaurant *Café Vogue* with its long menu, as well as a few bars and a club where soul, funk and Latino are king.

Diversity rules in *Piekarnia* at No. 11 Młocińska Street, groups and DJs both Polish and foreign performing here, the music coming from all corners of the world.

Organza, a club at No. 4 Sienkiewicza, is advertised as an enclave for those wishing to escape everyday life. In the evenings the DJs play moody chill-out music, while at the weekends an additional hall is opened for clubbers.

The superbly-located *Le Madame* club at No. 12 Koźla Street near Freta Street is the centre of underground and independent music. It offers 'monodramas', spectacles performed by a single artist, and plays put on by young theatre troupes from other Polish cities.

Last but by no means least, techno is the order of the day at the *CDQ* club at No. 22 Burakowska Street.

Discos

One of the most popular discos is *Quo Vadis* which is located at the Palace of Culture and Science, it plays commercial music, is large and usually full despite the high prices.

A weekend of disco music may be spent at the *Tango&Cash* club on *Aleje Jerozolimskie,* which has a huge floor and small bars on each level.

Classic disco is the specialty of *Park* at *Aleja Niepodległości 196.* Various kinds of music are played according to the day of the week: on Mondays, dance music, on Thursdays, metal. The club is inexpensive and quite safe.

One of Warsaw's first clubs was *Ground Zero* at No. 62 Wspólna Street, founded by two Americans at the site of the old nuclear shelter connected to the Palace of Culture and Science by means of an underground passage. A variety of rhythms may be enjoyed here and various events are organised, with both Polish and foreign stars invited to perform.

Lokomotywa, located in an old foundry at No. 37-39 Kolejowa Street, is a grand disco for techno music fans with moderately-priced drinks.

Clubbing in *Lokomotywa*

The *Stodoła* disco cannot be forgotten, a place of great tradition at No. 10a Batorego Street where the generations of students were entertained. A tradition that still continues. The repertoire is mainly rock and pop, although different styles do also feature.

Dancing and Casinos

An evening of dance with live music, appetisers and alcoholic beverages was one tradition of communist Warsaw which is now, however, almost extinct. On occasion, dancing in this old style is organised on Marszałkowska Street at the *Budapest* restaurant, while the restaurant at *Gromada* also tries to recall it too – at weekends this usually quiet establishment fills with dancers in their 50s or 60s.

Warsaw has a lot to offer gamblers, risk-takers and those tourists just tempted by the casinos at the *Marriott* and *Polonia* on *Aleje Jerozolimskie* or at the *Gromada* hotel on Powstańców Warszawy Square.

Other such 'hazardous' locations are found at the hotels of the *Orbis* chain; the *Grand* on Krucza Street and the *Sofitel Victoria Warsaw* on Królewska Street.

From spring to autumn luck may also be tested at the horse races held at *Służewiec*, an attraction for horse racing fans wishing to have a flutter.

Outdoor Events

In summer, on Warsaw's squares and in its parks, many outdoor events take place, for instance students at the city's universities participate in an event called the *Juvenalia* on the fields at *Agrykpola* or *Pola Mokotowskie*.

However, one of the most exciting events takes place in January, the *Great Orchestra of Christmas Charity* concerts, when money is collected for charitable causes. Thousands of people turn out on Parades Square and in front of the home of Polish Radio and Television on Woronicza Street in the Mokotów quarter.

Less emotional events, though still interesting, are the great historic shows. On Nowy Świat visitors may watch oddly-uniformed devotees reconstructing the November night of 1830 when a group of military school students marched to the *Belweder* palace to declare the November Uprising. Another great performance connected with this rebellion is the heroic battle of *Olszynka Grochowska* organised in Skaryszewski Park in the Praga quarter, a battle that

The *Hybrydy* club attracts young Varsovians

A jazz concert at the *Tygmont* club

saw Polish light cavalry up against Russian soldiers from St Petersburg. Great care is taken on the details, with historians of the Museum of the Polish Army being consulted and the combatants being re-enacted by history fans from Poland, Russia and Lithuania.

Sadly, festivals focused on the old and colourful Slavic customs are no longer popular, except with school groups and tourists, although Slavic traditions remain a feature of trade fairs where herbs, talismans and honey may sometimes be found.

Autumn is the season of ecological picnics and *Earth Day* an opportunity for the activists of ecological clubs to get their message of environmental protection heard.

Casino at the Marriott Hotel

At the time of the darkest communism, Warsaw was known for its most original Eastern European festival at which the grandest stars participated. Now the most prestigious festival of an international standard is the *Jazz Jamboree*, an idea born at the *Hybrydy* club in 1958 and begun by a few fans of jazz. In September of that year a very modest festival took place at the *Stodoła* students' club, the festival's name given by the leader of the Polish beatniks, the writer and ideologist Leopold Tyrmand. Soon the concerts were being organised at the National Philharmonic and since 1965 have been held at the Congress Hall of the Palace of Culture and Science. The biggest foreign stars taking part have so far been Duke Ellington, Miles Davis, Thelonius Monk, Dizzy Gilespie, Dave Brubeck, Benny Goldman and the Manhattan Transfer; participating Polish musicians have included Nahorny, Urbaniak, Stańko and Muniak, who during their concerts mastered their sound to equal the world's leading jazzmen. The Polish composer Krzysztof Komeda-Trzciński also refined his art at the *Jazz Jamboree* and went on to compose the famous lullaby for *Rosemary's Baby*.

Warsaw reinforces its image as the Slavic capital of jazz by organising a wide range of jazz events and concerts. The *Warsaw Summer Jazz Days* were created in the early 1990s; while the *Jazz Jamboree* is the event

where good old jazz is performed, the *Jazz Days* provide a stage for all of the newest trends. The festival takes place at the end of June in the Congress Hall and one day before the closing concert a great outdoor event is put on.

In the Old Market Square, the *International Outdoor Jazz Festival* is organised, which over two months attracts thousands of people – admission is free. Foreign and Polish artists take part, the main target of the event being the promotion and popularisation of various styles and trends in jazz, whether mainstream, swing, fusion, Latin, ethno or modern; many of the performers become big hits. The total audience is 40,000 listeners a year, making this the biggest music event in Poland, while in Europe only the *Paris Jazz Festival* is longer. Summer 2004 saw the tenth such event.

For several years Warsaw has hosted concerts of the *Era Jazz* Festival which was born in Poznań. The idea behind this festival is mobility, the reason it moves from place to place and the Varsovian concerts are held in the Congress Hall and at the National Philharmonic.

By the Vistula, even Chopin's music is played to a jazz rhythm. At the *Chopiniana* Festival on *Pola Mokotowskie* jazz musicians present brilliant improvisations.

Jazz clubs allow for jam sessions as

Left: the Tomasz Stańko Quartet at the 2004 Tenth International Outdoor Jazz Festival in the Old Town
Bottom: a Kahil El'Zubar concert during the Era Jazz festival

well as concerts, at which musicians improvise and compete in a relaxed atmosphere. However, these clubs have their ups and downs. Several years ago, the building housing the *Akwarium* club was demolished and replaced by a new skyscraper. *Remont* on Waryńskiego Street was luckier, which despite having suffered constant remodelling still serves the students of the Technical University. Newly-established clubs continue the traditions of the older ones, such as *Tygmont,* which hosts most festivals organised by the publishers of the prestigious *Jazz Forum* magazine.

Children

Among its tourist attractions Warsaw has much to offer families with small children. There are plays for the young and also films at the three-dimensional Imax cinema, while outside, hackney carriages and rickshaws bring the Old and New Towns closer in a fun way. Wheeled trains and road trains travel through the city, an additional form of recreation which complements the traditional kinds, such as playgrounds in parks or a visit to the zoo.

A scene from *The Ducklings' Kidnap*

Theatres/Cinemas/Philharmonic

Plays for children are staged at the *Bajka, Lalka* and *Guliwer* theatres and at *Studio Animacji,* although other theatres offer musicals. The Imax cinema is perhaps most worthy of attention as a place where the imagination is stimulated by various special effects. Tickets cost 10-20PLN for the theatre and cinema and 20-30PLN for the National Philharmonic *(Filharmonia Narodowa).*

Filharmonia Narodowa,
ul. Sienkiewicza 10,
Tel: + 48 22 551 71 39;
Baj, *ul. Jagiellońska 28,*
Tel: + 48 22 818 08 21;
Guliwer, *ul. Różana 16,*
Tel: + 48 22 845 16 76;
Lalka, *pl. Defilad 1*
(Palace,Tel: + 48 22 620 49 50;
Studio Animacji, *ul. Światowida 18,*
Tel: + 48 22 811 60 14;
Kino trójwymiarowe IMAX,
ul. Powsińska 31,
Tel: + 48 22 550 33 33.

Aqua Parks

Aqua parks appeared in Warsaw just a few years ago and offer heated swimming pools, artificial rivers and currents, water whips and geysers – children enjoy their slides, water mushrooms and wading and children's pools. Admission is currently 8-15PLN for 30min.

Kryta pływalnia OSiR, *ul. Rokosowska 10, Tel: + 48 22 572 90 70;*
Prawy Brzeg, *ul. Jagiellońska 7, Tel: + 48 22 619 81 38*
Prawy Brzeg *ul. Potocka 1, Tel: + 48 22 832 46 00;*
Wodnik, *ul. Abrahama 10, Tel: + 48 22 673 82 25;*
Wodny Park, *ul. Merliniego 4, Tel: + 48 22 854 01 30.*

The Zoo/Parks/Playgrounds

Animal lovers should visit Warsaw's Zoo where animals from every continent have their home. In the Łazienki gardens between spring and autumn children may take a gondola tour of the palace pond and see its ducks and swans, go for a pony ride or wagon tours. All year round peacocks walk the paths and squirrels jump from tree to tree and run on the lawns.

The colourful and fragrant Botanical Gardens is also worth a look *(see Parks and Gardens see p94)*, while Warsaw also offers playgrounds like *Kolorado* which is full of slides and pools of coloured balls, and there is also a Minizoo, an Indian village and many other attractions prepared especially for children by *Entertainment Park Pepeland* in Łomianki. Recently many special halls have been built where children may play.

The Zoo, *ul. Ratuszowa 1/3,*
Tel: + 48 22 619 40 41;
The Warsaw University Botanical Garden, *Al. Ujazdowskie 4,*
Tel: + 48 22 553 05 23;
The Botanical Garden in Powsin, *ul. Prawdziwka 2, Tel: + 48 22 648 38 56;*
Kolorado *ul. Konarskiego 88,*
Tel: + 48 22 36 11 51;
Pepeland
Entertainment Park,
Łomianki,
ul. Kolejowa 378,
Tel: + 48 22 751 26 27;
Bajlandia, *ul. Samolotowa 4,*
Tel: + 48 22 672 41 51;
Eldorado, *ul. Powstańców Śląskich 126,*
Tel: + 48 22 569 72 69;
Hokus Pokus, *ul. Powsińska 31,*
Tel: + 48 22 550 35 35;
Kids Play, *ul. Sójki 37,*
Tel: + 48 22 644 41 44.

Wheeled Train Tours/Views/Exhibitions

Children enjoy journeys on the wheeled train called Tschu-tschu which runs every 30 minutes on Zamkowy Square, through the streets of the Old and New Towns – in summer a 50-minute tram tour starts on Strynkiewicza Square. A viewing platform is located on the 30th floor of the Palace of Culture and Science, accessed by a rapid elevator, while the Museum of Technology, Palace of Culture and Science and Ethnographic and Archeological Museums organise art classes *(see Museums and Galleries p100).*

Wheeled Train Tschu-tschu,
reservations; Tel: + 48 0501 131 245;
Tourist tram, *Tel: + 48 22 843 14 51;*
Warsaw Panorama (30th floor of the Palace of Culture and Science),
Tel: + 48 22 656 77 35;
Viewing terrace at Okęcie Airport,
Tel: + 48 22 650 40 76.

The Fairy Tale Zoo, a favourite place with Warsaw's children

Sport

There are many options for active relaxation in Warsaw and a great number of sports centres, with new swimming pools, aqua parks, tennis courts, golf courses and cycle routes laid out. In addition to this, climbing walls and skiing centres have been established in Szczęśliwice, watersports are popular on Zegrzyński Reservoir near the city and horse-riding centres are found both within Warsaw and on its outskirts.

One of the numerous bowling alleys

Walking and Biking Trails

The peripheral districts of Warsaw provide many opportunites for walking and cycling tours, with the area of Kampinoska Woodlands being particularly attractive, along with the green quarters of Wawer, Wilanów, Ursynów and Białołęka. The most popular cycle trail, and the longest, is the Vistula Route (*Szlak Wisły*), which is about 37km in length. It starts at the Kampinoska Woodlands and runs along the Vistula in the direction of the Łazienki Gardens before following Belwederska and Sobieskiego Streets to Powsin. Other routes include the Sun Trail (*Szlak Słoneczny*; 8.5km), leading from Grota-Roweckiego Bridge to Łazienkowski Bridge, the Circuit Trail (*Szlak Obwodowy*; 21.4km), which joins Na Rozdrożu Square with Bielany, the Battles of Warsaw Trail (32.7km) and in the city centre the trail leading along the Varsovian Scarp (*Podskarpowa Ścieżka Rowerow*; about 5km).

The Warsaw Marathon, a popular sporting event held in September

Swimmings Pools/Water sports

Aqua parks (see *Children* p158-9) and
indoor swimming pools, not to mention
the outdoor swimming pools opened in
the summer season, give the active visitor
plenty of options. Every district has its
own pool and their addresses are given in
leaflets published by the local Tourist
Information Office. Beyond such facilities,
watersport centres are located on the
Zegrzyński Reservoir where colourful
regattas are organised in summer and
autumn and rental shops opened in high
season.

Tennis/Golf/Bowling/Squash/Paintball

Tennis courts may be found in
Skaryszewski Park (No. 2 Zieleniecka
Street), at Legia stadium (No. 4a
Myśliwiecka Street), at *Skra* (No. 5
Wawelska Street) and at the Warsaw
Sports Centre (No. 71 Solec Street). Golf
courses are located in the suburbs in the
town of Rajszew (No. 70 Rajszew,
Jabłonna) and at Golf Parks Poland (No. 1
Vogla Street). Bowling is offered at sports
centres and aqua parks at No. 10
Abrahama Street, No. 71 Solec Street, No.
31 Powsińska Street and No. 4 Merliniego
Street as well as at a number of shopping
centres. Similarly squash has become
more popular and courts are to be found
at No. 71 Solec Street, No. 34
Marymoncka Street and No. 4 Merliniego
Street. Group paintballing is provided
near the *IMOLA* go-kart track at No. 33
Puławska Street in Piaseczno as well as in
the city itself at No. 10 Widok Street and
No. 18/5 Klaudyny Street.

Horse-riding/Horse Races

Horse-riding centres are located in the

Warsaw's Aqua Park

suburbs, but also closer to the centre.
They are *CWKS Legia* (No. 4a Kozielska
Street), *IGAMI* (No. 378 Kolejowa Street)
and *Podkowa* (No. 11 Głogów Street) in
Dziekanów Leśny, *Stangret* Horse-riding
School (No. 2 Wybrzeże Gdańskie Street)
and St George's Stable in Aleksandrów
near Warsaw. Horse-racing fans have the
exciting Sunday competition at the
Słuńewiec racetrack.

Winter Sports

Hockey and figure skating competitions
take place at *Torwar* (No. 6a
Łazienkowska Street) and speed skating at
the *Stegny* rink (No. 1 Inspektowa Street),
although recreation is also possible there.
Skiing is possible year-round at the Ski
Centre in the Szczęśliwice district, at No.
22 Drawska Street; the length of the ski
run is about 227m, with a vertical drop of
about 44m and an average inclination of
21 percent.

Food and Drink

Warsaw offers food for all; those eating on the move as well as those seeking new culinary experiences. Warsaw is home to international chain restaurants such as McDonalds and KFC yet the city is also able to offer a range of international cuisines, and although prices vary, a meal can be found to suit every budget. The sole problem is which establishment of the 600 in the city to choose from!

Summer decorations in front of Barss

What to eat

In Warsaw, meals from all corners of the world may be tried. Poles hungry for novelties tend to visit the restaurants offering more exotic dishes; a few years ago the most popular dish was pizza, now the crowds gravitate towards *sushi*. Among the restaurants specialising in international cuisines the most popular is *fusion,* the key to which is the blending of various culinary traditions in one dish.

For many years Polish cuisine was regarded as boring and heavy but it has now regained faithful fans. Upon this renaissance of all things traditionally-Polish, numerous restaurants have built their popularity, offering dishes that were once served in the manors of the nobility. Also popular are the regional cuisines based on inexpensive ingredients.

What to drink

Poland is famous for its excellent white and coloured vodkas which may be enjoyed in bars and restaurants specialising in Polish cuisine. Particularly precious are those vodkas prepared according to recipes hundreds of years old.

Also worthy of recommendation is mead, or *miód pitny,* a truly old-Polish beverage. The most notable is the amber-coloured *półtorak*, which is one part honey to one half water and is bottled after six years in a cellar. Additional buckwheat honey and fruit juices are added to develop the fragrance. The mead named *dwójniak,* one part honey to one part water, is matured for several years too, while *trójniak* at two parts water to one part honey is matured for two years; the driest is the mead named *czwórniak* which matures for just a single year. For a personal assessment of their qualities, a *miodosytnia* is recommended, which is a venue where mead is served, for example *Pasieka*.

Despite the traditions of vodka and mead, the most popular beverage is beer, or *piwo,* which is served in Warsaw's numerous pubs and summer beer gardens in the parks and alongside the Vistula river. As a rule, wine is not produced in Poland although wineries are popular and the majority of Italian, French and Spanish restaurants offer good wines; Hungarian and Bulgarian brands are well worth trying too.

Where to eat

In Warsaw there ought to be no difficulty in finding space in a proper place to eat because the Poles do not generally dine at restaurants, traditional home-made meals being habitual. Warsaw offers meals for all kinds of traveller and at every standard.

Hungry travellers on a long sightseeing trip may simply step in to an international chain restaurant (for example McDonald's or KFC) for relatively cheap if unsophisticated meals. Beyond this, the streets of the capital are full of booths and bars selling the so-called *zapiekanka* alongside other simple dishes, and a rapid meal, particularly early in the afternoon, may be had in those bars which offer a lunch menu.

The more discerning may try one of the few hundred restaurants offering almost

Restaurant in the New Town

every kind of culinary tradition. The largest number of restaurants is of course to be found in the city centre, yet restaurants located further out, even on the outskirts, can be recommended too. Please note that many restaurants fill up with tourist or business people visiting the city, so making a reservation is often wise.

Cafés

Varsovians love meeting in cafés where coffee, cakes and ice-cream desserts are all served. The most popular are the more stylish, such as those belonging to the renowned *Blikle* and *Wedel* families.

Vegetarian Cuisine

Not so long ago finding a vegetarian restaurant in Warsaw was a stunning achievement. However, the growing popularity of mediterranean meals and changing Polish eating habits have forced restaurants to offer meals not only based on meat, with stricter vegan dishes often available too. The smaller restaurants usually offer such dishes at reasonable prices.

The Oriental restaurant, Sheraton Hotel

Restaurants

The number of stars indicates the average cost of a three course-meal, half a bottle of a house wine and service (in Polish *zloty*, or PLN).

★ up to 50PLN
★★ 50-80PLN
★★★ 80-120PLN
★★★★ 120-160PLN

Absynt ★★★

ul. Wspólna 35,
Tel: + 48 22 621 18 81.
A cosy French restaurant with two halls offering classic French dishes and several original dishes.

Adler ★★

ul. Mokotowska 69,
Tel: + 48 22 628 73 84.
Its interior furnished with heavy wooden furniture

Adler offers Bavarian dishes and a variety of beers. In summer an outdoor garden is opened.

Bangkok ★★

ul. Kopińska 10b,
Tel: + 48 22 668 94 93.
Oriental cuisine is to be found on the menu here, particularly Thai.

Bar & Grill Chicago's

★★ *ul. Żelazna 41,*
Tel: + 48 22 890 09 99.
A small restaurant serving Polish beer and simple grilled dishes. On Saturdays, there is live music.

Bazyliszek ★★★

Rynek Starego Miasta 3-9,
Tel: + 48 22 831 18 41.
In this spacious and well-furnished restaurant,

international and old Polish dishes are served, with concerts held in the evenings.

Casa Valdemar ★★★

ul. Piękna 7-9,
Tel: + 48 22 628 81 40.
Stylish, this is one of the best Spanish restaurants in Warsaw. It offers fresh oven-baked dishes, while seafood may be selected direct from a glass tank. Live flamenco concerts are held in the evenings.

Chianti ★★★

ul. Foksal 17,
Tel: + 48 22 828 02 22.
An Italian trattoria serving delicious meals with excellent wines. Serenades are also sung here.

The interior of the popular Mexican restaurant *El Popo*

Dom Polski ★★★★
ul. Francuska 11,
Tel: + 48 22 616 24 32.
This villa in Saska Kępa
has a traditional interior
with solid and comfortable
furniture and embroidered
tablecloths. *Tatar* made of
horse meat and a *żur* soup
based on the broth of a
wild mushroom called
borowik are popular.

El Popo ★★★
ul. Senatorska 27,
Tel: + 48 22 827 23 40.
The best Mexican
restaurant in Warsaw. Spicy
dishes and traditional
beverages such as tequila
and margherita are served
and a stay is made more
pleasant by the Latino
music.

Flik ★★★ *ul. Puławska 43,*
Tel: + 48 22 849 44 06.
A cosy and elegant
restaurant near Morskie
Oko park. Polish dishes
rule here, but international
dishes are also available. In
summer an outdoor garden
is available.

Folk Gospoda ★★
ul. Walicóш 13,
Tel: + 48 22 890 16 05
Folk bands play here in
rustic interiors. Particularly
recommended are the
placki ziemniaczane with

The entrance to the renowned restaurant *U Fukiera*

soured cream, bigos á la
farmer (*bigos po chłopsku*)
and oven-baked *golonka*,
or pork shank. Typical
farmers' beverages are also
worth trying, for example
Orzechóшka, or green
walnut vodka.

India Curry ★★★
ul. Żurawia 22,
Tel: + 48 22 816 13 90.
In the elegant interiors
here Indian dishes are
served, and in the evenings
guests may watch
Bollywood films.

Kamala ★
ul. Nowy Świat 64,
*Tel: + 48 22 0 503 187
779.*
A two-storey restaurant
with ethnic cuisine and live
music and dance
performances.

Karpielówka ★★
ul. Indiri Ghandi 11,
Tel: + 48 22 644 85 10.
In interiors modelled on a
Zakopane highlander's
cottage, a guest at
Karpielówka may try
starters including the home-
made *smalec* and grilled
oscypek cheese, with main
courses including *bigos*
served in bread or with
potatoes. All taste better
with the live music.

Mirador ★★★
ul. Grzybowska 2,
Tel: + 48 22 436 35 35.
A Spanish restaurant
belonging to the famous
Kręglicki family of
restaurateurs. Diners here
may try vegetable paella,
aubergine stuffed with wild
rice, kurki wild mushrooms
with garlic and parsley.

Pierrogeria ★

ul. Chłodna 39,
Tel: + 48 22 654 84 44.
A restaurant offering the
typically Polish, home-
made *pierogi*, flattish
dumplings with various
fillings, for example
chicken with wild
mushrooms; *pierogi* are
hand-made before being
baked in the oven.

Tradycja ★★★

ul. Belwederska 18a,
Tel: + 48 22 840 69 01.
A stylishly-furnished
restaurant offering old
Polish dishes and superb
desserts where guests may
enjoy live music.

Prowansja ★★

ul. Koszykowa 1,
Tel: + 48 22 621 42 58.
Elegant Provence-themed
interiors in earthy colours
make this restaurant
resemble a summer house
of the French region; it
offers mediterranean
cuisine and a wide
selection of excellent
wines.

Qchnia Artystyczna

★★★★ *Al.Ujazdowskie 6,*
Tel: + 48 22 625 76 27.
This restaurant is located
at Ujazdowski Palace
and offers international
cuisine. In summer a

Fruit and vegetables in the garden of an Old Town restaurant

terrace is available.

Restauracja Kurta Schellera ★★★★

ul. Wilcza 73,
Tel: + 48 22 584 87 71.
The owner of this
restaurant, the famous
Swiss cook Kurt Scheller,
invites diners for classes at
his Academy of Cooking,
the school having its own
timetable and the option of
different types of cuisine
and dish. Cooking takes
place under the guidance
of Kurt Scheller himself,
and later students are
welcome to eat with the
Swiss master.

Ryżowe Pole - Sushi Bar

★★ *ul. Zgoda 5,*
Tel: + 48 22 556 47 37.
A small restaurant with a
sushi lunch menu, a few

warm dishes and Japanese
instrumental music.

Sadhu Café ★★★ *ul. Wałowa 3,*

Tel: + 48 22 635 81 39.
Timber furnishings and a
roaring fire provide this
restaurant with its
atmosphere, while the
dishes served can be
enjoyed by the most
orthodox vegetarians.
Smoking is forbidden.

Samira ★ *Al. Niepodległości 213,*

Tel: + 48 22 825 09 61.
An oriental snack-bar
located away from the busy
downtown at Pola
Mokotowskie which serves
up Lebanese and Indian
cuisine.

Santorini ★★★ *ul. Egipska 7, Tel: + 48 22 672 05 25.* Situated at the pavilion in Saska Kępa, this restaurant has the character of a real Greek tavern, its Greek dishes enjoyed by the fussiest eaters. An attraction is the covered patio.

Sense ★★ *ul. Nowy Świat 19, Tel: + 48 22 826 65 70.* This restaurant specialises in fusion cuisine, blending oriental tastes with European.

St. Patrick's Irish Pub ★★ *ul. Nowogrodzka 31, Tel: + 48 22 817 13 39.* This venue has the character of a typical Irish pub; St Patrick's Day is celebrated with vigour.

Tam tam ★★★ *ul. Foksal 18, Tel: + 48 22 828 26 22.* With interiors inspired by African climes, Tam tam offers a wide array of meat and fish dishes originating in various cultures. In summer guests may dine in the garden outside the restaurant.

U Fukiera ★★★★ *Rynek Starego Miasta 27, Tel: + 48 22 831 10 13.* A restaurant located in an Old Town townhouse, the specialty of which is old

Polish cuisine. The interiors are decorated with bunches of herbs and meadow flowers and musicians play while seated on the inner patio.

U Szwejka ★★ *pl. Konstytucji 1, Tel: + 48 22 621 62 11.* A restaurant offering Czech national cuisine as well as international dishes.

Warszawa-Jerozolima ★★★★ *ul. Smocza 27, Tel: + 48 22 838 3217.* This restaurant specialises in dishes of Jewish, Israeli and Polish cuisines, the singing waiters making a meal here especially enjoyable.

Cafés

Café Antykwariat ★ *ul. Żurawia 45, Tel: + 48 22 629 99 29.* A small café where cake and coffee are provided together with jazz music, and where guests may thumb through the books standing on shelves.

Café Blikle ★ *ul. Nowy Świat 33, Tel: + 48 22 826 66 19.* This café belongs to the famous Blikle family of confectioners. In its cosy interior coffee and tea are

served with incomparable cakes, including the mouth-watering glazed *pączki* with their rose jam filling.

Café Bristol ★★ *ul. Krakowskie Przedmieście 42-44, Tel: + 48 22 551 18 28.* Located at the stylish Bristol hotel, this café is known for its savoury desserts and rather high prices.

Café Strauss ★★ *Al. Jerozolimskie 45.* A refined café at the Polonia Palace hotel with a typically Viennese arrangement. Desserts and a variety of coffees are served here.

Pijalnia Czekolady Wedla ★ *ul. Szpitalna 1.* In the two urban-furnished rooms of the Chocolate Drinking House adjoining Wedel's sweet shop, guests may try the famous hot chocolate, drink coffee or enjoy a superb dessert. This is a place visited by the next generation of Varsovians.

Pożegnanie z Afryką ★ *ul. Freta 4-6, Tel: + 48 22 831 44 20.* This café is also a shop selling various brands of coffee.

The earliest cafés were established at the time of the Wettin dynasty in the 18th century. The Varsovian palate was conquered first by the royal confectioner Lessel, who managed the buffet in the Saski Gardens, and later by the Swiss Lourse, whose specialties were French puff pastries, croissants with an almond filling and the Napoleon puff pastry *(Napoleonka)* with *grillage* or cherry jam. Lourse had managed a French café on Miodowa Street since 1821 and later managed one at the *Europejski* hotel on Krakowskie Przedmieście.

The Blikle family also has a long history in the confectionery business. Their company was established in 1869 at No. 35 Nowy Świat by A Blikle and was active up until the Warsaw Uprising. Today the Blikle café is an elegant meeting place where a blend of South American and African coffee is served along with home-made cakes and pastries or with a cake called the *Florentynka*. The Polish

nation celebrates Shrove Thursday rather than Shrove Tuesday and on that day long queues form for the Blikle's famous *pączki* with their rose jam filling.

Another magical place is the old-fashioned Chocolate Drinking House, or *Pijalnia czekolady Wedla*, on Szpitalna Street. Karl Vedel, the first of the chocolate dynasty, arrived in Warsaw in 1845 and in 1851 opened a café on Miodowa Street, four years later he began chocolate production using a steam engine imported from France. In the 1890s Emil Wedel moved production and sale to the newly built eclecticist house on Szpitalna Street, where the shop and *pijalnia* are still active, selling Wedel's delicacies and serving chocolate. The list of chocolate products has become ever longer over the years, yet some of the originals remain to this day; the *Jedyna* chocolate bar even retaining its wrapper design. Wedel's family built a modern factory in 1931 in the Praga quarter which is still in operation, its rich aromas filling the area.

Warsaw is also famous for ice cream. For the post-war generations the name *Zielona Budka* (Green Booth) has been synonymous with ice cream of the highest quality. Although the Green Booth in question stood on Puławska Street in Warsaw,

the firm's history began
not in the Polish
capital, but in Buczacz
in Ukraine where
Grzegorz Grycan and
his son Jozef made and
sold ice cream. When
Buczacz became Soviet
in 1945 the Grycan
family moved to
Wrocław, the capital of
the province of Lower
Silesia, where Weronika
Grycan opened the first
ice cream parlour in Poland on
Wrocław's Grunwaldzki Square with a
sign reading *Lody Miś. Zbigniew*. They
sell cacao, vanilla, coffee, strawberry,
woodland strawberry
(poziomkowe) and lemon ice
cream. They also offered ice
cream Penguins *(pingwin)*
which was quite possibly
the first Polish ice cream to
come on a stick.

Of the Grycan family's third
generation, was a trainee at
Warsaw's Bristol hotel who, after
he became a fully-qualified
confectioner, bought the family
business and developed it
into a great factory and chain of
shops, bringing this wonderful ice
cream into the majority of Polish homes.
However, owing to financial problems
Zbigniew Grycan sold the company to
Roncadin GmbH, only to become

dissatisfied with the changes made by
the new owners. As a result, he left the
company to found a new ice cream
factory, *Grycan - Lody od Pokoleń*,
meaning 'Ice cream for Generations'.

Now Warsaw is home to the ice
creams of both *Zielona Budka*
and *Grycan*, and each and every
visitor should discover for
themselves the answer to the
problem, which is the better!

*Ice Cream Parlour Firmow, 11
Puławska Street;*
*Arkadia Shopping Centre, 82 Jana
Pawła II Avenue;*
*King Kross Shopping Centre, Jubilerska
Street 1/3;*
*Redunta Shopping Centre, 15
Głebocka Street*

Left: Blikle's *pączki* with their rose jam filling
Middle right: an ice cream dessert
Upper right: a counter filled with sweets at the
Wedel shop

Hotels and Accommodation

Since 1989 the number of hotels in Warsaw has increased, with completely new luxurious hotels having been built as well as older ones modernised. Besides these at the top end, less expensive tourist-class hotels have been established so that Warsaw can now offer about 20,000 places to stay. Budget travellers and students may make use of several student hostels *(hotel studencki)* while visitors who prefer their personal space can stay in an apartment.

The entrance to the exclusive *Polonia Palace* hotel

Hotel Prices

Prices at the more exclusive 4- or 5-star hotels are 560-1700PLN for a single room, 50 percent more for a double, while at 2- or 3-star hotels the price range is 300-600PLN for a single, then at tourist-class hotels the prices are somewhat lower, at 15-60PLN per night. At youth hostels prices are 15-60PLN per night, in guest houses 35-70PLN for a single room, 50-100PLN for a double. Less expensive still are campsites. A list of hotels and youth hostels is included at p174.

Location

The most convenient option is to stay in the city centre, in the area of Krakowskie Przedmieście not far from the Old Town, or on Piłsudskiego Square, Marszałkowska Street or Aleje Jerozolimskie where there's a lot to see and good access to shops and restaurants. The city centre is dominated by more expensive hotels offering a higher standard, although there are also a number of mid-range hotels, for instance the *Metropol* on Marszałkowska Street and the *Grand* on Krucza Street, some hotels of tourist standard, like the *Mazowiecki* hotel on Długa Street, and guest houses or apartments such as *Dom Literatury* on Krakowskie Przedmieście. There are youth hostels on the New Market Square and Myśliwiecka Street, and several comfortable hostels have been built outside of Warsaw too, although their distance makes them less popular.

Reservations

Warsaw suffers from a lack of cheaper hotels, a reason that reservations should be made a few weeks in advance for busy times: June and July through September and even up to November; this is also true for higher quality hotels. Tourist offices assure visitors that they will all find a bed, but in fact finding one can be problematic. A list of booking offices may be found on p174.

Rooms for travellers with disabilities

Ever more Varsovian hotels are introducing facilities for guests with disabilities. Rooms adapted to the needs of wheel-chair users are available at both 4- and 5-star hotels and even at the cheaper 1- or 2-star hotels, tourist-class hotels, youth hostels and rented summer dormitories. Hotels with rooms for guests with disabilities are marked with 'N' in the accommodation list on p174-5.

Discounts for Children

Beds may be added to rooms and restaurants may offer a children's menu, higher chairs and smaller tables, while babysitters may also be available. Some hotels offer special prices or free accommodation for children under three. It is worth asking about the availability of a family room when making a reservation.

Hotel Types

The luxurious city centre hotels are the most popular, hotels like the *Bristol* on Krakowskie Przedmieście, with its preserved secession interiors, the modern *Sheraton* on Trzech Krzyży Square or the glass-domed *Jan III Sobieski* Hotel on Zawisza Square, famous for its dining. The main disadvantage of those hotels belonging to international chains are their lack of original furnishings and atmosphere. However, such qualities may be found in smaller hotels located further from the centre, such as *Zajazd Napoleoński* (The Napoleon Inn) on Płowecka Street.

Worthy of note are the small hotels located in newly-renovated houses or office blocks, or the 'employee hotels' remembering communism, among them *Reytan, Portos, Atos* and *Aramis* in the Mokotów district. At the tourist-class hotels en-suite bathrooms are standard, although shared bathrooms may sometimes be encountered.

The budget tourist and youthful traveller

A room at the *Jan III Sobieski* hotel

may like to try a room at a students' dormitory *(akademik)*, which are available mainly in summer.

Hotel staff do speak foreign languages, most often English.

Guest Houses

The popularity of guest houses is growing, particularly as they are often located in the centre yet with prices below 100PLN for a double room. However, the price usually excludes some services, for example breakfast. Outside of the city centre, guest houses located along the underground line are a good choice, that is from the Żoliborz to the Ursynów and Kabaty districts, as travel to the centre is faster. Visitors may settle their bill in cash or by money transfer at an agency, taking the receipt as proof of payment.

Apartments

Accommodation in apartments is new to Warsaw and has become popular with Polish and foreign tourists alike. Their main advantage is their location in the city centre and Old Town, while they are smaller and give greater privacy too. Despite being rather luxurious, they are usually comparable in the price of a double room to a hotel. Apartments are an excellent option, particularly for longer stays or for large families.

Youth Hostels

Warsaw possesses seven youth hostels open year-round, offering inexpensive accommodation in shared rooms. Their good locations and low prices make them popular with school groups who often organise tours in the May-June and September-October periods, a reason for pre-booking, especially at weekends.

The fashionable JP's bar at the Westin hotel

These hostels are managed according to the rules laid down by the International Youth Hostel Federation.

Campsites

There are two campsites located about 8km east of the centre, one at No. 15-17 Bitwy Warszawskiej 1920 Street and the other at No. 1 Grochowska Street. In the area of Okęcie Airport, there is a campsite at No. 3-5 Żwirki i Wigury Street, while in Powsin close to Warsaw is a camp situated in a wood in the area of the Botanical Garden which opens from April to October. These sites offer space for tents, buses, campervans or caravans, with shower blocks and even rooms in cottages. More detailed information is available at Tourist Information Centres.

Accommodation around Warsaw

Warsaw's numerous suburban hotels offer a base where home-made dishes are complemented by scenic locations. One such hotel is *Konstancja* in Konstancin-Jeziorna, located close to the brine graduation towers, which offers campfire talks and horse riding. Another is *Eden* in Raszyn, not far from the *Janki* Shopping Centre and famous for its excellent cuisine. A third, about 15km from Warsaw in Józefów, is the *Beauty Secret Farm*, which specialises in active tourism and therapeutic facilities; the microclimate benefits respiratory system conditions, while walking and cycling trails run through the Mazovian Landscape Park. Prices in all of these places are similar to those of mid-range hotels.

An apartment at the Sheraton Hotel

Reservation Offices

Warsaw and Home Accommodation Information,
Mon - Sun 10am–5pm,
Tel: +48 22 641 53 66;
Mon - Sat 5pm–10pm,
Tel: +48 22 662 64 89.
Capital Office of Promotion and Information,
Tel: +48 22 94 31; www.warsawtour.pl,
e-mail: info@warsawtour.pl.

Private Accommodation Office in PHT Syrena,
ul. Krucza 17,
Tel: +48 22 628 75 40,
Mon - Fri. 9am–7pm,
Sat - Sun. 1pm–7pm.
Almatur,
ul. Kopernika 23,
Tel: +48 22 826 35 12,
every day 9am-6pm
Information on accommodation at students' dormitories, open in summer.

Exclusive Hotels
(4- and 5-star)
Bristol Le Royal Meridien, *ul. Krakowskie Przedmieście 42-44,*
Tel: +48 22 551 10 00, N.
An elegant hotel with a rich history and two excellent restaurants, Marconi and

Malinowa. Guests have free access to a swimming pool and sauna, steam bagnio and fitness club.

Holiday Inn,
ul. Złota 48-54,
Tel: +48 22 697 39 99, N.
A renowned hotel with a conference and banquet hall.

Hyatt Regency Warsaw,
ul. Belwederska 23,
Tel: +48 22 558 12 34, N.
Attractively located on the Royal Tract.

Jan III Sobieski,
pl. A. Zawiszy 1,
Tel: +48 22 579 10 00, N.
A prestigious hotel with an internal garden and furniture of cherry wood. Famous for its cooking and facilities for businessmen, such as a modern business centre.

Marriott,
Al. Jerozolimskie 65-79,
Tel: +48 22 630 55 28, N.
Luxurious furnishings, five restaurants and a casino.

Mercure Fryderyk Chopin,
al. Jana Pawła II 22,
Tel: +48 22 620 15 21, N.
A modern hotel with three restaurants, Le Balzac offering French cuisine.

Novotel Centrum,
ul. Nowogrodzka 24-26,
Tel: +48 22 621 02 71, N.
The former Forum hotel, refurnished to become one of the first modern hotels of a high standard in the city.

Rialto,
ul. Wilcza 73,
Tel: +48 22 628 46 22, N.
A small hotel with a good restaurant.

Sas Radisson,
ul. Grzybowska 24,
Tel: +48 22 321 88 88, N.
A hotel with a number of facilities for guests, including a beauty centre and restaurants.

Sheraton Warsaw Hotel & Towers,
ul. Prusa 2,
Tel: +48 22 657 68 00, N.
Four restaurants covering Polish, Asian and international cuisines, modern furnishings and a well-equipped business centre.

Sofitel Victoria,
ul. Królewska 11,
Tel: +48 22 657 80 11, N.
Three restaurants offering Polish and international cuisines, a business centre, an indoor swimming pool, a beauty centre and a casino.

Old Town Apartments,
Rynek Starego Miasta 12-14,
Tel: +48 22 887 98 01,
826 09 29, N.
Comfortable and quiet apartments well-located in the cultural heart of the capital.

Mid-range Hotels (2- and 3-star)

Airport Okęcie,
ul. 17 Stycznia 24,
Tel: +48 22 456 80 00, N.

A modern hotel near the airport.

Belwederski,
ul. Sulkiewicza 11,
Tel: +48 22 682 26 66
Not big, known for excellent service and good meals.

City Apartments Warsaw,
ul. Hoża 38,
Tel: +48 22 628 76 11.
Well-located apartments in refurnished houses, with the option of staying at a hotel.

Dipservice Apartments Zgoda,
ul. Zgoda 6,
Tel: +48 22 553 62 00.
An alternative for the tourist wishing to feel in Warsaw as if in their own home.

Grand Orbis,
ul. Krucza 28,
Tel: +48 22 583 22 00.
A city centre hotel located in a social-realist building.

Centralny Hotel Gromada,
pl. Powstańców Warszawy 2, Tel: +48 22 582 99 00.
A well-situated venue with a good conference and business centre.

Harenda,
ul. Krakowskie Przedmieście 4-6,
Tel: +48 22 826 00 71.
The choice of those carrying backpacks for its good location, but a hotel which also offers low prices and pleasant service.

Maria,
al. Jana Pawła II 71,
Tel: +48 22 838 40 62.
A small hotel, stylishly
furnished with cosy
rooms.

Metropol,
ul. Marszałkowska 99a,
Tel: +48 22 621 10 93.
While this hotel's exterior
may not be attractive, its
interior is.

Novotel Orbis,
ul. 1 Sierpnia 1,
Tel: +48 22 575 63 45, N.
A hotel close to Okęcie
Airport at which animals
are welcome.

Solec Orbis,
ul. Zagórna 1,
Tel: +48 22 625 44 00.
A hotel situated close to a
park by the Vistula.

**Warsaw Apartments
Sadyba**,
ul. Augustówka 9,
Tel: +48 22 651 74 64.
Luxurious apartments
close to the Wilanów
quarter.

The Westin Warsaw,
ul. Jana Pawła II 21,
Tel: +48 22 450 80 00.
A modern hotel in the city
centre, visitors attracted by
the lift running in a glass
tube which seems to be
attached to the building.

Tourist-class Hotels
Amicus Dom
Pielgrzyma,
ul. Hozjusza 2,
Tel: +48 22 561 00 00.
A house popular with
pilgrims.

Aramis,
ul. Mangalia 3b,
Tel: +48 22 642 96 35, N.
Atos, *ul. Mangalia 1,*
Tel: +48 22 841 10 43.
Portos,
ul. Mangalia 3a,
Tel: +48 22 642 75 35, N.
Three twin hotels located
near the Royal Tract.

Dom Literaty,
ul. Krakowskie
Przedmieście 87-89,
Tel: +48 22/fax 828 39 20.
An excellent location;
inexpensive and cosy.

Harctur,
ul. Niemcewicza 17,
Tel: +48 22 822 19 13.
An inexpensive hotel
offering good meals.

Logos,
ul. Wybrzeże
Kościuszkowskie 31-33,
Tel: +48 22 622 89 92.
A former hotel for teachers
with a café, buffet and
bar.

Mazowiecki,
ul. Mazowiecka 10,
Tel: +48 22 687 91 17.
A hotel with solid
furniture, not overpriced
despite a city centre
location.

Around Warsaw
Beauty Secret Farm,
Józefów, ul. Nowowiejska
38,
Tel: +48 22 789 20 16.
Accommodation with
home-made meals and a
modern beauty farm.

Konstancja,
Konstancin Jeziorna, ul.

Źródlana 6-8,
Tel: +48 22 756 43 25.
A good location for active
relaxation, with horse-
riding and evening talks
around the campfire.

Eden, *Raszyn, ul.*
Mszczonowska 43,
Tel: +48 22 756 05 22.
A place offering
comfortable rooms and
pleasant service along
with old-Polish cuisine.

Youth Hostels
Syrenka,
ul. Karolkowa 53a,
Tel: +48 22 632 88 29.
Agrykola, *ul. Myśliwiecka*
9, Tel: +48 22 622 91 10,
N.

PTSM,
ul. Międzyparkowa 4,
Tel /fax: +48 22 831 17 66
(open 1st April – 31st
October).

Przy Rynku,
Rynek Nowego Miasta 4,
Tel: +48 22/fax 831 50 33
(open 23rd June – 31st
August).

On Business

One of Warsaw's modern office blocks

Since the political changes of 1989 Warsaw has become a business centre and is now a place of international congresses and trade fairs, most held in the Palace of Culture and Science. Poland's accession to the European Union and the increasing competitiveness of the Polish economy have also influenced the development of modern Warsaw. Detailed information on Polish business is available at the offices of auxiliary organisations, daily newspapers and dedicated magazines.

Business Hours

The Polish working day is 8 hours long and the working week runs from Monday to Friday. Government agencies work 8am-4pm, 9am-5pm or 10am-5pm, and in some institutions employees have half-hour lunch breaks. Banks, common in every district of Warsaw, open longer hours, from 8am to 7pm.

Conference Centres

Specialist conference centres are located in Warsaw as well as in towns nearby, such as Jabłonna, Jadwisin, Jachranka, Raszyn, Serock and Nowy Dwór Mazowiecki. In the city such centres are found at the Palace of Culture and Science and at the historical palaces in Jabłonna and Jadwisin. Although Warsaw has no single large conference venue, the Palace of Culture and Science most often plays this role, and the newer conference centres are located in modern buildings with air-conditioned rooms, simultaneous interpreting equipment, microphones and multimedia facilities, as well as accommodation, restaurants, cafés and fitness clubs; however, all conference equipment is also available at other smaller or older hotels.

Addresses of agencies providing conference services, training courses or team-building events are listed below:

Centrum finansowe - (The Financial Centre), *ul. Puławska 15,*
Tel: + 48 22 521 66 66, fax 521 66 65,
e-mail: c.konferencyjne@cfp.com.pl,
www.cfp.com.pl

Centrum konferencyjne w Jadwisinie - (The Conference Centre in Jadwisin),
Tel: + 48 22 782 75 08, fax 782 67 31,
www.owjadwisin.pl

Centrum szkoleniowo-konferencyjne - (The Training and Conference Centre),
Warszawa Miedzeszyn, ul. Odrębna 4,
Tel : + 48 22 612 77 90, fax 872 06 80,
e-mail: dyrekcja@centrumsk.pl,
www.centrumsk.pl;

The Lord Hotel,
Warszawa Okęcie, Al. Krakowska 218,
Tel: + 48 22 574 20 20, fax 574 21 21,
e-mail: okecie@hotellord.com.pl,
www.hotellord.com.pl;

Bea Conference Service,
Nowy Dwór Mazowiecki, ul. Spacerowa 4,
Tel /fax: + 48 22 713 33 36,
www.bea-konferencje.com.pl;
Pałac Kultury i Nauki -
(The Palace of Culture and Science),
pl. Defilad 4,
Tel: + 48 22 656 61 41, fax 656 62 08,
e-mail: zarzad@pkin.pl, www.pkin.pl.

The Stock Exchange

Warsaw's Stock Exchange *(Warszawska Giełda Papierów Wartościowych SA)* was founded in 1991 and soon became the largest in Central and Eastern Europe. It first home was the communist party building on the corner of Jerozolimskie Avenue and Nowy Świat, although at present the exchange is situated at No. 4 Książęca Street *(Tel: +48 22 628 32 32, www.gpw.com.pl)*, the same building hosting the National Shares Deposit *(Tel: + 48 22 537 94 68)*.

Organisations and Business Magazines

Information on organisations and institutions involved with business in Warsaw may be obtained from the **Business Centre Club** *(pl. Żelaznej Bramy 10, Tel: + 48 22 625 30 37, www.bcc.org.pl)* and **Polish Confederation of Private Employers (Polska Konfederacja Pracodawów Prywatnych,** *ul. Klonowa 10, Tel: + 48 22 845 95 50,*

...... *prywatni.pl)*. Organisation of and business travel is dealt **Warsaw Convention Bureau** 26, Tel: + 48 22 629 07 50, 14, e-mail:web@warsawtour.pl, *wtour.pl)*, which acts under es of the local authorities and is by the **Polish Tourist tion (Polska Organizacja zna)**. Business-related issues are by specialist magazines and by ents provided with daily ers such as *Rzeczpospolita,* *Wyborcza* and *Gazeta Prawna.* ition on the stock exchange is published in *Parkiet*, banking reports and analysis are published in the financial monthly *Bank*, the finances of Polish companies are described in *Finansista* and articles, analysis and reviews regarding the economy are published in *Puls biznesu*. The popular weeklies *Polityka, Newsweek* and *Wprost* and the monthly *Businessman Magazine* and *Profit* also deal with business issues.

The House under Eagles and a branch of BPH bank

Practical Guide

Customs and foreign exchange

A Polish visa is not obligatory for the
majority of citizens arriving from the
European Union (EU) or even beyond;
however, as Poland is a member of the EU
those citizens requiring a visa for entry to
the countries of the EU also require one
for Poland.

There are no restrictions as to the
number of items for personal use brought
into Poland. Special permission is needed
for a weapon to be brought to Poland and
for export of antiques. Non-EU citizens are
obliged to observe the regulations limiting
the quantities of cigarettes and alcohol
brought to Poland. Since 1st May 2004 the
unified customs law of the EU has been in
force; detailed information is available at
Customs Information at Okęcie Airport
*(Tel: +48 22 650 34 80, +48 22 650 34
31).*

A plane taking off at Okęcie Airport

By plane

In the terminal at Okęcie Airport there are
travel agents, a bank, currency exchange
offices and cash points, as well as a post
office, souvenir shops, a restaurant, a bar,
a tourist information centre and car hire.
The domestic airport *(lotnisko krajowe)* is
located nearby. Warsaw's city centre may
be reached by means of the No. 175 bus,
while the No. 188 bus route links the
airport with the right bank of the city,
South Praga. Three taxi corporations, *MPT,
SAWA* and *MERC,* have their offices in the
middle of the Arrivals hall and offer
services for fixed prices; more beneficial is
to call for a taxi (see *Taxis p184-5*).

By train

Warsaw has three railway stations serving
international destinations and long-
distance domestic traffic: *Warszawa
Centralna, Warszawa Wschodnia* and
Warszawa Zachodnia. The centrally-
located *Warszawa Centralna* at No. 54
Jerozolimskie Avenue has good bus and
tram connections with other districts and is
close to an underground *(Metro)* station
and the well-connected *WKD Warszawa
Śródmieście* train station. In the main hall
of *Warszawa Centralna* is a tourist
information centre, a pharmacy, a post
office, a currency exchange office, cash
points, a train information office and bars.

Travellers aiming for Warsaw's right
bank should head to *Warszawa
Wschodnia,* while travel to the left bank
of the city is possible from *Warszawa
Zachodnia; Zachodnia* is joined by an
underground passage to the *PKS* bus
station at No. 144 Jerozolimskie Avenue,

Warsaw's largest such hub and the one serving both domestic and international destinations.

By car

Poland's border crossings operate 24 hours a day. Foreign driving licences are valid in Poland, but while driving a car a visitor should have this licence with them as well as the car's registration documents. If the car is rented, the documents proving this are required. Poland suffers from a shortage of motorways and fast routes; the speed limit on motorways is 130km/h, on fast routes 100km/h and outside of towns 90km/h. Travel throughout Poland is free in that road tax is included in petrol prices, the exception being the paid A2 motorway between Konin and Poznań and the A4 between Katowice and Kraków, where a charge of about 10PLN is made.

Weather

Warsaw's climate is one of extremes. Summer may bring roasting heat with occasional heavy downpours, while the frost is quite severe in January and February; lately however, winters have been light without excessive snow- or rainfall. Spring and autumn are seasons of strong wind, while autumn shares with winter a lack of strong sunlight.

Crime

Car theft can be a problem in Warsaw and even for short stays a car should be left in a guarded car park if possible, all valuables being taken out or at least well hidden. In some trams and buses, such as those of route 175 from the airport to the city centre, pickpockets are the problem, entering the vehicle in groups to form an

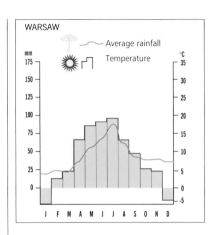

artificial crowd. Theft can occur on some streets and at railway stations, particularly on the right bank of Warsaw in the area of Brzeska Street, Różycki's Bazaar and the *Warszawa Wschodnia* and *Stadion* railway stations, also at bus stations.

Driving in Warsaw

Warsaw's rush hours are 7am-9am and 2pm-5pm, when the capital may well become jammed. The level of traffic can be influenced by both weather conditions and construction work. The next issue is finding a free parking space. In Warsaw as in other built-up areas it is permissible to drive at up to 50km/h between 6am and 11pm, and at up to 60km/h between 11pm and 6am.

Driving Safely

The minimum age for driving in Poland is 18 years of age. In Poland seat belts must be fastened (taxi drivers and pregnant women being exceptions to the rule) and children younger than 12 years of age are not permitted to sit in a front seat. If a taxi has rear seat belts it is obligatory for passengers to fasten them. Between 1st November and 1st March drivers must use headlights all day and night. Poland has very rigorous rules regarding drinking alcohol and driving. The limit is 0.2 mg/ml (blood/alcohol).

Car Hire

Car hire costs around 200-250PLN per day in Warsaw, with hire shops situated at Okęcie Airport, the *Marriott Hotel* and in many other locations in the centre. One hire firm operating 24 hours a day is Rent a Car Poland *(ul. Marszałkowska 140, Tel: + 48 22 826 71 00)*, while at the airport the following firms are found: *Avis (Tel: + 48 22 650 48 72), Budget (Tel: + 48 22 650 40 62), Global Poland (Tel: + 48 22 650 14 83), Hertz (Tel: + 48 22 650 28 96, www.hertz.com.pl)* and *National Car Rental (Tel: + 48 22 606 92 02)*. At the *Marriott Hotel* are *Avis (Tel: + 48 22 630 73 16), Budget (Tel: + 48 22 630 72 80)* and *Five (Tel: + 48 22 629 75 15)*. There is also the *Avis* Central Booking Office *(Centralna Rezerwacja, Tel: + 48 22 0*

The entrance to an Old Town pharmacy

801 120 010, www.avis.pl).

Petrol and Parking

Besides petrol stations *(stacja benzynowa)* belonging to Polish companies like *Orlen* and *Petrochemia,* there are stations selling the petrol of better-known concerns, for example *Shell* and *Statoil*. The frequency of petrol stations is high and prices vary, but one litre of diesel fuel currently costs around 3PLN, petrol with an octane level of 95 *(benzyna 95 oktanowa bezołowiowa or 98)* is also available currently at 3.60-3.80PLN.

Parking in Warsaw is charged only in marked zones; a 15-minute stay currently costs around 0.50PLN and a 30-minute stay 1PLN, while one hour costs around 2.60PLN and each subsequent hour an additional 2.60PLN.

Health and Insurance

Warsaw offers both public and private health care. Unfortunately only first aid is free, which is why it is extremely beneficial (if not crucial) to take out insurance to cover the cost of any medical treatment. Foreign visitors are treated at local hospitals and should have their passports with them; without insurance, money to pay the bill is necessary, although it is possible to ask for an invoice and pay later. Health care information is also available: *Private Health Care, Tel: + 48 22 827 89 62; Daily Medical Information, Tel: + 48 22 94 39*.

Emergency Telephone Numbers

In the event of a life-threatening situation call: Integrated Rescue System: 112 from a mobile

Police *(Policja): free 997, 826 24 24, 669 99 97*
Emergency Medical Service *(Pogotowie Ratunkowe): free 999, 525 12 99*
Fire Brigade *(Straż Pożarna): free 998, 844 00 71*
Warsaw's City Guard *(Straż miejska): free 986, 840 0016, 840 34 15*
Roadside Assistance *(Pomoc drogowa): free 981, 96 33.*

The Lost Property Office

If documents become lost, the Lost Property Office *(Biuro Rzeczy Znalezionych)* may be checked *Tel:* + 48 22 619 56 68

Money/Exchanging Money/Credit Cards.

The currency unit in Poland is the ZŁOTY (zł), each of which is divided into 100 GROSZ (gr). Notes come in 10, 20, 50, 100 and 200zł denominations, coins in 1, 2 and 5zł and 1, 2, 5, 10, 20 and 50gr. Travellers may exchange money at a bank or currency exchange office *(Kantor Wymiany Walut).* It is definitely worth checking the exchange rate and commission charged. Credit cards are also popular and accepted at larger shops, petrol stations, hotels, restaurants and travel agencies.

The currency unit in Poland is the ZŁOTY (zł), each of which is divided into 100 GROSZ (gr). Notes come in 10, 20, 50, 100 and 200zł denominations, coins in 1, 2 and 5zł and 1, 2, 5, 10, 20 and 50gr. Travellers may exchange money at a bank or currency exchange office (Kantor Wymiany Walut). It is definitely worth checking the exchange rate and commission charged. Credit cards are also

popular and accepted at larger shops, petrol stations, hotels, restaurants and travel agencies.

Banks and Currency Exchange Offices

The majority of banks are located in the city centre and allow all financial operations to be performed.

One of Warsaw's parkometers

They are generally open from 8am to 7pm on weekdays, although some only until 6pm; at lunchtime queues are usually longer. On Saturdays some banks open until 2pm. Currencies can be exchanged at a *Kantor,* or Currency Exchange Office, some of which are run daily, as is the one at the *Centralny* railway station. Currency exchange offices offer a better exchange rate, particularly at night and on Sundays when the rate becomes lower. Currencies may also be exchanged at hotels, which do charge commission for this service. It is never advisable to exchange money on the street.

Embassies and Consulates

Although there are consulates located in other big cities like Krakow or Gdańsk, Warsaw is home to all of the embassies in Poland, the majority situated in the city centre in the area of Ujazdowskie Avenue. The addresses of all of the embassies are listed on the website of the Ministry of

Foreign Affairs (MSZ) at www.msz.gov.pl; it is also possible to call the MSZ information centre *Tel: + 48 22 523 90 00* or check the phone book at a post office.

The Media - the Press, Television and Radio

Magazines and newspapers available in Warsaw include the two nationwide newspapers, *Gazeta Wyborcza* and *Rzeczpospolita*, the free newspapers, *Metro* and *Metropol*, which are handed out on the street, the weekly *Polityka*, *Newsweek* and English-language *Warsaw Voice* *(www.warsawvoice.pl)* and the magazines mentioned on p177. News for Warsaw and the Mazovia region are published in *Życie Warszawy*, in supplements in the nationwide newspapers and in the afternoon newspaper *Super Express*. Newspapers may be bought in kiosks, newsagents and EMPIK stores, the latter also stocking foreign titles. Hotels may also offer a monthly newsletter in foreign languages.

Public Television *(Telewizja Polska)* broadcasts programmes on two nationwide channels, *TVP1* and *TVP2*, the regional *TVP3* with information on Warsaw itself and Mazovia, and a channel for Polish citizens living abroad broadcast via satellite, *TVP Polonia*. Other popular programmes are broadcast on the private channels *TVN, TVN 24* and *Polsat, TVN 24* providing information in English several times a day. Foreign tourists usually opt for the music stations of the nationwide public Polish Radio *(Polski Radio), PR 1, PR 2, PR 3, Radio Bis* and *Radio Polonia*.

There are also around 220 private radio stations, the most popular being *RMF FM, Radio ZET, Radio Kolor* and *Wa-Wa*.

The Internet

The Internet has become immensely popular in private homes and in workplaces and is becoming accessible from hotels, guest houses and clubs too. Those without their own access may make use of one of the numerous Internet cafés *(kawiarenka internetowa)*.

Maps

Detailed maps are available in kiosks and bookshops or at tourist information centres, with the latter offering free maps of the city centre too. It is strongly recommended that new maps are used as many street and square names have been changed since the days of communism when streets and squares for example were named after famous communists or revolutionaries.

Opening Hours

Grocery stores *(sklep spożywczy)* are usually open from 7am until 7pm, but recently many supermarkets have begun opening from 9am until 9pm and *TESCO* supermarkets are open 24 hours a day. Shops located in the areas of housing estates are open until 10pm or even all day long. Boutiques, home appliances shops and clothing and footwear shops are open from 10am until 7pm, although some open at 11am and close at 8pm.

Museums are open from Tuesday to Saturday 10am-5pm, on Sundays one or two hours less; Mondays are a free day.

Exact opening hours may be gleaned from newspaper or magazine supplements, such as *Co jest grane* in Friday's edition of *Gazeta Wyborcza*.

Public and Church Holidays

Some institutions, banks and shops do open on Saturdays or Sundays. Polish national and church holidays are as follows:
New Year - 1st January; Easter Monday - variable; Labour Day - 1st May; Constitution or 3rd May Day - 3rd May; Corpus Christi (*Boże Ciało*, a feast day, some roads may be closed) - variable, in June; The Assumption of the Holy Mother of God - 15th August; All Saints' Day - 1st November; Independence Day - 11th November; Christmas - 25th-26th December.

Police

Police officers wear uniforms when policing the streets and patrol the city in navy-blue and white cars with *POLICJA* emblazoned across the doors along with the number of the unit. These road patrols are permitted to stop cars to check their condition and the sobriety of their driver. The Polish Border Police Service (*Służba Graniczna*) is also allowed to stop and check cars and have almost the same rights as police officers in terms of road policing.

In Poland driving after drinking more than the minimal amount of alcohol (0.2 mg/ml (blood/alcohol), or making use of any substance acting similarly, is not tolerated and the penalties for drink driving are very high. The best method of communication with the police is a visit to the police station (*komisariat*).

Post Offices

Post offices (*Poczta*) are open from Monday to Friday 8am-7pm and on Saturdays some are open between 8am-2pm; the Main Post Office (*Poczta Główna, ul. Świętokszyska 31-33*) is open daily. At a post office letters and parcels can be sent, phonecards bought and money transfers made, while at a special stand for philatelists collectable postal stamps may be bought. In some post offices customers are asked to take a ticket with a number to order the queue.

Sustainable Tourism

Thomas Cook is a strong advocate of ethical and fairly traded tourism and believes that the travel experience should be as good for the places visited as it is for the people that visit. That is why Thomas Cook is a firm supporter of The Travel Foundation, a charity that develops solutions to help improve and protect holiday destinations, their environment, traditions and culture. To find out what you can do to make a positive difference to the places you travel to and the people who live there, please visit www.thetravelfoundation.org.uk.

Telephoning

Calling from a phone box requires a phonecard (*karta telefoniczna*) with a chip, the price depending on the number of 'impulses' bought. Connections are most expensive between 8am and 10pm and cheapest on Sundays and public holidays. For connections with the national provider *TP SA*, '0' is dialled, followed by the area code and number; for non-*TP* connections '0' is followed by the special prefix of the phone operator, the area code and the number. A yellow phone allows e-mails and text (SMS) messages to be sent, and the yellow *Karta SMS TP* provides about 20 messages for 5PLN.

A phone call may also be purchased at a post office with payment made after completion. Depending on the zone being called such connections currently cost from 2.14 to 8.78PLN per minute. Calls made from hotels are much more expensive than those from a phone box.

Time

Warsaw lies in the CEST (Central European Summer Time) zone; between March and the end of September daylight saving time is used.

Cloakrooms/Tipping

Cloakrooms in hotels and restaurants usually charge a fee and waiters, porters and maids do expect to be tipped. However, Varsovians usually only give a few *zloty*, and even then for exceptional standards.

The Municipal Transportation System

On buses and trams travellers are obliged to be in possession of a ticket with the words *ZTM Warszawa* printed on it, which may be bought at all kiosks stocking newspapers or from the driver with a 0.50PLN surcharge. A ticket is only valid if it is punched/validated immediately after boarding, in the device attached to a vertical handrail; on the underground tickets must be punched on the platform. Tickets for trams, buses and

the underground are identically priced. Currently regular single tickets cost around 2.40PLN (concessionary price 1.20PLN or 1.25PLN); night tickets and tickets to suburban areas of the city cost 4.80PLN; timed regular 24-hour tickets (valid 24 hours from their punching) are 7.20PLN (concessionary price 3.60PLN or 3.70PLN); three-day tickets (valid three days from their punching, including night bus fares) are 12PLN (concessionary price 6PLN or 6.20PLN; weekly (valid seven days from their punching) are 24PLN (concessionary price 12PLN or 12.40PLN). The surcharge for certain amounts of luggage or an animal is equal to the value of one regular ticket, while the fine for travelling without a valid ticket is 120PLN; concessionary tickets are solely for use by school and university students, the retired and those living on a pension. More information is available from *ZTM* (*Tel:* +48 22 94 84, *www.ztm.waw.pl*).

Free Fares

Since 2005 public transport users over seventy have been able to travel for free. The user must carry a document confirming their age. In Poland some children may also travel for free, though only those below seven who are not primary school students.

Travellers with Disabilities

Disabled travellers may either travel free of charge or are entitled to fare reductions of 50% and can usually expect help from other commuters; the underground offers the best conditions. Information on this issue may be obtained by calling, *Tel:* +48 22 94 84, *www.ztm.waw.pl*.

Those wishing to travel more

independently are advised to contact the *Tus Foundation (Fundacja Tus, Tel: +48 22 831 93 31, e-mail: tus6@wp.pl)* or the university transport service *(Tel: +48 22 552 42 24)*.

Taxis for those with disabilities are offered by *MPT TAXI (Tel: +48 22 919), SUPER TAXI (Tel: +48 22 96 22), SAWA TAXI (Tel: +48 22 644 44 44) and ELE TAXI (Tel: +48 22 811 11 11)*.

Taxis

Varsovian taxis have a yellow-and-red stripe with the city's coat of arms, a number and a rooftop lamp with the word 'TAXI'. However, there are taxis in other colours belonging to different corporations, and some hotels have their own taxis too, although this latter group are quite expensive. Taxis booked by telephone are up to 50% cheaper.

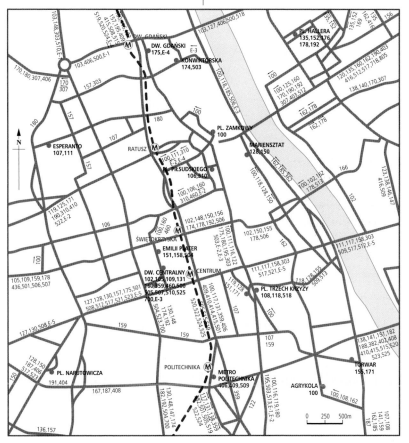

Warsaw's bus routes and underground

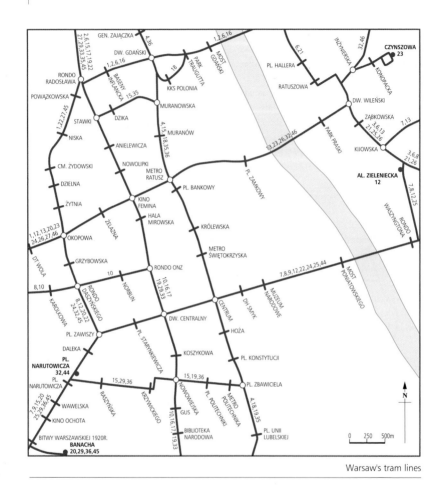

Warsaw's tram lines

When picking up a taxi on the street it is a good idea to ask the price per kilometre as the differences are substantial. The daytime fare within the city is currently about 1.40-3PLN per kilometre, on Sundays and official holidays 4.50PLN; 6PLN per kilometre is the daytime tariff beyond the city boundary. At night the tariff within Warsaw is 4.50PLN per kilometre, rising to 9PLN per kilometre in suburban areas and on Sundays and holidays. Additional costs include 6PLN from the moment that you embark while 40PLN is charged for an hour of waiting. Some taxi corporations accept credit cards, for instance *MPT TAXI, SAWA TAXI* and *SUPER TAXI.*

Toilets

Public toilets are rare in Warsaw, and

those existing do not enjoy a European standard of hygiene. Toilets in the majority of eating establishments require payment, though not in such places as *McDonald's* or *KFC*. The charge is usually 1-2PLN, but is clearly posted. Toilets adapted for wheel chair users are mainly located at 4- or 5-star hotels, yet they may also be found in some theatres, restaurants, libraries and sport centres.

Tourist Information

Warsaw's Tourist Information Centres give free and detailed information on culture, trade fairs, tourism and recreation, and guides and car hire within Warsaw and beyond. Tourism publications on the city are also available along with maps, guidebooks and albums.

These centres also sell the Warsaw Tourist Card *(Warszawska Karta Turystyczna)*, which is available in a 24-hour or 3-day version. This card allows tourists to use the municipal communication system for free, provides admission to twenty museums, gives discounts in galleries, accommodation and sport centres, and when buying tours in and around Warsaw, hiring a car and paying in a restaurant and selected shops and entertainment venues.

For information *Tel: +48 22 94 31*, by e-mail to *info@warsawtour.pl* or at *www.warsawtour.pl*.

Tourist Information Centre - Central Railway Station (main hall), No. 54 Jerozolimskie Avenue. Open: May-September 9am-8pm; October-April 9am-6pm every day.

Tourist Information Centre - F Chopin International Airport at Okęcie (Arrivals), Żwirki i Wigury Street. Open: May-September 9am-8pm; October-April 9am-6pm every day.

Tourist Information Centre - Western PKS Bus Station *(Dworzec Zachodni PKS)* next to the ticket offices, No. 144 Jerozolimskie Avenue. Open: 9am-5pm every day.

Tourist Information Centre – Krakowskie Przedmiescie No. 39. Opening hours TBA.

The entrance to an underground station

Acknowledgements

Hachette Livre Poland would like to thank the following individuals and institutions who have given their permission for the publication of photographs that they own:
Krystyna Bartosik - the National Ethnographic Museum, Kamila Gawędzka - Fabryka Trzciny Artistic Centre, Agnieszka Horbaczewska - Santorini, Kuba Kamiński - Czuły Barbarzyńca, Agnieszka Koperniak - Muranów Cinema, Sebastian Madejski - Zachęta Gallery, Ewa Magiera - the Home Office of the Director of Citizens' Platform (PO), Katarzyna Michalak - the Jan III Sobieski Hotel, Bartosz Nagórny - Warsaw Underground, Dionizy Piątkowski - Director of the Era Jazz Festival, Paweł Pokora - the Dramatyczny Theatre, Małgorzata Potocka and Beata Trochimiuk - Sabat Theatre, Wojciech Rohoziński - Director of the F Chopin Airport, Sylwia Stawska - the Sheraton Hotel, Jolanta Tuchowska, Krzysztof Wojciechowski, Ewa Ziółkowska - Warsaw Zoo, Katarzyna Żebrowska - Luksfera Gallery, The Director of the Aqua Park, Cinema City Poland, Hybrydy, The Director of the Jazz in the Old Town Market Square Festival, Lokomotywa, The Mokotów Gallery, The National Philharmonic, The promotions department of the Modern Art Centre at Ujazdowski Palace, The Guliwer Puppet Theatre, The Museum of Warsaw Uprising, The Museum of Asia and the Pacific, Tygmont, The Warsaw Marathon Foundation.

Hachette Livre Poland would also like to thank the following individuals whose photographs were used in this publication:
Andys (page 155), Jadwiga Antoniak (page 95), Maria Betlejewska (pages 70, 74), Czesław Czapliński (page 151), Krystyna Dąbrowska (page 60), Eugeniusz Helbert (page 102 top), Jan Jagielski (page 120 top), Maciej Janaszek (page 160 bottom), Kuba Kamiński (page 20 top), Wojciech Kryński (pages 11, 43, 51 top, 51 bottom, 63, 80, 98 bottom), Sebastian Madejski (page 101), Katarzyna and Wojciech Mądrzak (pages 23 top, 147), Mariusz Michalski (page 100 bottom), Stefan Okołwicz (page 20 bottom), Jakub Pajewski (page 168), Tomasz Paruch (page 153), Katarzyna Raince (page 157), Wojciech Rohoziński (page 178), Jacek Sielski (page 102 bottom), Maciej Skoczeń (pages 104, 105), Krzysztof Wojciechowski (page 156), Andrzej Zawadzki (page 152), Ewa Ziółkowska (pages 136 bottom, 159), Ewa Maria Ziółkowska (page 15 top).

Sources of the remaining photographs:
Aqua Park Archive (page 161), Cinema City Poland Archive (page 150), Citizens' Platform (PO) Archive (page 16), Eugeniusz Lokajski's Archive (page 14), Fabryka Trzciny Archive (page 145), Hybrydy club Archive (page 154), Jan III Sobieski Hotel Archive (page 171), Jewish History Institute Archive (pages 116 bottom, 123 top). Luksfera Gallery Archive (page 144), Mokotów Gallery Archive (page 149), National Philharmonic Archive (page 23 bottom), Sheraton Hotel Archive (pages 163, 172, 173), Siesta Archive (page 164), The Museum of Asia and Pacific Archive (page 102 top), The National Ethnographic Museum Archive (page 102 bottom), Warsaw Underground Archive (page 26 bottom), Casinos Poland (page 155 bottom).

Feedback Form

Please help us improve future editions by taking part in our reader survey. Every returned form will be acknowledged. To show our appreciation we will send you a voucher entitling you to £1 off your next *Travellers* guide or any other Thomas Cook guidebook ordered direct from Thomas Cook Publishing. Just take a few minutes to complete and return this form to us.

We'd also be glad to hear of your comments, updates or recommendations on places we cover or you think that we ought to cover.

3. Which of the following tempted you into buying your *Travellers* guide:

(Please tick as many as appropriate)

a) the price ☐

b) the cover ☐

c) the content ☐

d) other _____

2. What do you think of:

a) the cover design _____

b) the design and layout styles within the book_____

c) the content_____

d) the maps _____

3. Please tell us about any features that in your opinion could be changed, improved or added in future editions of the book or any other comments you would like to make concerning this book_____

_____

_____

_____

_____

4. What is the single most useful/helpful aspect of this book?_____

_____

cut along the dotted line

5. Have you purchased other *Travellers* Guides in the series?

a) yes ☐

b) no ☐

If Yes, please specify which titles _____

6. Would you purchase other Travellers Guides?

a) yes ☐

b) no ☐

If No, please specify why not _____

Your age category: ☐ under 21 ☐ 21-30 ☐ 31-40 ☐ 41-50 ☐ 51+

Mr/Mrs/Miss/Ms/Other

Surname_____ Initials_____

Full address: (Please include postal or zip code)_____

_____

_____

Daytime telephone number: _____

E-mail address:_____

Please detach this page and send it to: **The Series Editor, Travellers Guides,
Thomas Cook Publishing, PO Box 227, The Thomas Cook Business Park,
Units 15-16, Coningsby Road, Peterborough PE3 8SB, United Kingdom.**

Alternatively, you can e-mail us at: *books@thomascook.com*